MW01089438

Williams College

Williamstown, Massachusetts

Written by Alexandra Grashkina

Edited by Adam Burns, Kelly Carey,
Kimberly Moore, and Jon Skindzier

Layout by Carrie Petersen

Additional contributions by Omid Gohari,
Christina Koshzow, Chris Mason, Joey Rahimi,
and Luke Skurman

ISBN # 1-4274-0221-3
ISSN # 1552-1850

Last updated 5/16/2006

Special Thanks To: Babs Carryer, Andy Hannah, LaunchCyte, Tim O'Brien, Bob Sehlinger, Thomas Emerson, Andrew Skurman, Barbara Skurman, Bert Mann, Dave Lehman, Daniel Fayock, Chris Babyak, The Donald H. Jones Center for Entrepreneurship, Terry Slease, Jerry McGinnis, Bill Ecenberger, Idie McGinty, Kyle Russell, Jacque Zaremba, Larry Winderbaum, Roland Allen, Jon Reider, Team Evankovich, Lauren Varacalli, Abu Noaman, Mark Exler, Daniel Steinmeyer, Jared Cohon, Gabriela Oates, David Koegler, Glen Meakem, and the Williams College Bounce-Back Team.

College Prowler®
5001 Baum Blvd.
Suite 750
Pittsburgh, PA 15213

Phone: 1-800-290-2682
Fax: 1-800-772-4972
E-Mail: info@collegeprowler.com
Web Site: www.collegeprowler.com

How this all started...

When I was trying to find the perfect college, I used every resource that was available to me. I went online to visit school websites; I talked with my high school guidance counselor; I read book after book; I hired a private counselor. Sure, this was all very helpful, but nothing really told me what life was like at the schools I cared about. These sources weren't giving me enough information to be totally confident in my decision.

In all my research, there were only two ways to get the information I wanted.

The first was to physically visit the campuses and see if things were really how the brochures described them, but this was quite expensive and not always feasible. The second involved a missing ingredient: the students. Actually talking to a few students at those schools gave me a taste of the information that I needed so badly. The problem was that I wanted more but didn't have access to enough people.

In the end, I weighed my options and decided on a school that felt right and had a great academic reputation, but truth be told, the choice was still very much a crapshoot. I had done as much research as any other student, but was I 100 percent positive that I had picked the school of my dreams?

Absolutely not.

My dream in creating *College Prowler* was to build a resource that people can use with confidence. My own college search experience taught me the importance of gaining true insider insight; that's why the majority of this guide is composed of quotes from actual students. After all, shouldn't you hear about a school from the people who know it best?

I hope you enjoy reading this book as much as I've enjoyed putting it together. Tell me what you think when you get a chance. I'd love to hear your college selection stories.

Luke Skurman
CEO and Co-Founder
lukeskurman@collegeprowler.com

Welcome to College Prowler®

During the writing of College Prowler's guidebooks, we felt it was critical that our content was unbiased and unaffiliated with any college or university. We think it's important that our readers get honest information and a realistic impression of the student opinions on any campus—that's why if any aspect of a particular school is terrible, we (unlike a campus brochure) intend to publish it. While we do keep an eye out for the occasional extremist—the cheerleader or the cynic—we take pride in letting the students tell it like it is. We strive to create a book that's as representative as possible of each particular campus. Our books cover both the good and the bad, and whether the survey responses point to recurring trends or a variation in opinion, these sentiments are directly and proportionally expressed through our guides.

College Prowler guidebooks are in the hands of students throughout the entire process of their creation. Because you can't make student-written guides without the students, we have students at each campus who help write, randomly survey their peers, edit, layout, and perform accuracy checks on every book that we publish. From the very beginning, student writers gather the most up-to-date stats, facts, and inside information on their colleges. They fill each section with student quotes and summarize the findings in editorial reviews. In addition, each school receives a collection of letter grades (A through F) that reflect student opinion and help to represent contentment, prominence, or satisfaction for each of our 20 specific categories. Just as in grade school, the higher the mark the more content, more prominent, or more satisfied the students are with the particular category.

Once a book is written, additional students serve as editors and check for accuracy even more extensively. Our bounce-back team—a group of randomly selected students who have no involvement with the project—are asked to read over the material in order to help ensure that the book accurately expresses every aspect of the university and its students. This same process is applied to the 200-plus schools College Prowler currently covers. Each book is the result of endless student contributions, hundreds of pages of research and writing, and countless hours of hard work. All of this has led to the creation of a student information network that stretches across the nation to every school that we cover. It's no easy accomplishment, but it's the reason that our guides are such a great resource.

When reading our books and looking at our grades, keep in mind that every college is different and that the students who make up each school are not uniform—as a result, it is important to assess schools on a case-by-case basis. Because it's impossible to summarize an entire school with a single number or description, each book provides a dialogue, not a decision, that's made up of 20 different topics and hundreds of student quotes. In the end, we hope that this guide will serve as a valuable tool in your college selection process. Enjoy!

OMID GOHARI ◯ CHRISTINA KOSHZOW ◯ CHRIS MASON ◯ JOEY RAHIMI ◯ LUKE SKURMAN ◯
The College Prowler Team

Table of Contents

Introduction from the Author

Williams College is a very small school, so it is interesting that in the course of my education here, I am continually surprised. First, one might be shocked to learn that there is only one street in town where daytime and evening events occur. One might also be surprised to find that the key to a good nightlife lies in self-sufficiency. The academic and athletic rigors are also surprising, as well as the endless winter season. Surprisingly, the campus is even more beautiful, safe, and clean than it looks in pictures.

You will never cease to be amazed in your four years at Williams. This book intends to examine the heart and soul of a school that will always keep you guessing. Enjoy!

Alexandra Grashkina, Author
Williams College

By the Numbers

General Information

Williams College
988 Main St.
Williamstown, MA 01267

Control:
Private

Academic Calendar:
4-1-4

Religious Affiliation:
None

Founded:
1793

Web Site:
www.williams.edu

Main Phone:
(413) 597-3131

Admissions Phone:
(413) 597-2211

Student Body

**Full-Time
Undergraduates:**
1,953

**Part-Time
Undergraduates:**
38

**Total Male
Undergraduates:**
975

**Total Female
Undergraduates:**
1,016

Admissions

Overall Acceptance Rate:
19%

Regular Acceptance Rate:
17%

Total Applicants:
5,705

Total Acceptances:
1,093

Freshman Enrollment:
537

Yield (% of admitted students who actually enroll):
49%

Early Decision Available?
Yes

Early Action Available?
No

Early Decision Deadline:
November 10

Early Decision Notification:
December 15

Early Decision Acceptance Rate:
38%

Regular Decision Deadline:
January 1

Regular Decision Notification:
April 9

Must-Reply-By Date:
May 1

Transfer Applications Received:
79

Transfer Applications Accepted:
9

Transfer Students Enrolled:
4

Transfer Application Acceptance Rate:
11%

Common Application Accepted?
Yes

Supplemental Forms?
Yes, visit *www.williams. edu/admission/apply_ appinstructions.php*

Admissions E-Mail:
admission@williams.edu

Admissions Web Site:
www.williams.edu/admission/ apply.php

SAT I or ACT Required?
Either

SAT I Range (25th–75th Percentile):
1330–1520

SAT I Verbal Range (25th–75th Percentile):
660–760

SAT I Math Range (25th–75th Percentile):
670–760

Retention Rate:
97%

**Top 10% of
High School Class:**
85%

Application Fee:
$60

Financial Information

Tuiton:
$31,760

Room and Board:
$8,550

Books and Supplies:
$800

**Average Need-Based
Financial Aid Package
(including loans, work-study,
grants, and other sources):**
$27,840

**Students Who Applied
for Financial Aid:**
54%

**Students Who
Received Aid:**
42%

**Financial Aid
Forms Deadline:**
February 15

Financial Aid Phone:
(413) 597-4181

Financial Aid E-Mail:
finaid@williams.edu

Financial Aid Web Site:
*www.williams.edu/admission/
finaid.php*

Academics

The Lowdown On...
Academics

Degrees Awarded:

Bachelor

Master

Most Popular Majors:

16% Psychology

15% English Language
    and Literature

15% Economics

14% Political Science
    and Government

10% Art/Art Studies

→

Faculty with Terminal Degree:
96%

Student-to-Faculty Ratio:
8:1

Average Course Load:
4 classes

Graduation Rates:
Four-Year: 91%
Five-Year: 94%
Six-Year: 96%

Special Degree Options

3-2 engineering program, accelerated program, cross-registration, double major, exchange student program (domestic), honors program, independent study, student-designed major, study abroad, teacher certificate program

AP Test Score Requirements

Possible credit or class placement

IB Test Score Requirements

Scores of 5, 6, or 7 with particular attention paid to higher subject scores

Sample Academic Clubs

Phi Beta Capa, Sigma Xi

Best Place to Study

Schow Library

Did You Know?

The **first African American student** to graduate from Williams graduated in 1889.

Students Speak Out On...
Academics

> "Professors are definitely one of the best things about our school. They do their jobs so well, I have thought of becoming a professor myself."

Q "When I came to Williams as a freshman, everybody kept telling me that the French professors weren't really good. I had taken four years of French in high school and was intent on pursuing the language further. In four years, the department improved; they hired new professors and came up with new courses. I definitely don't regret majoring in French. I also know that many other majors here are even better than French, so I think that **no matter what you choose, you will learn a lot** at Williams. I don't think you should be declaring your major on the basis of a department's reputation, but rather on your true interests. Departments change every semester, and there is a lot of student input influencing these changes."

Q "Professors at Williams are very friendly, helpful, and knowledgeable. Most are very hard graders, though, so you will have to sweat for that A-. In the end, you know you have learned a lot to earn your grade. At Williams, **there isn't much pressure to have the highest GPA**, so professors are fair to their students, even though they set high standards. I know that I need some pressure in order to work hard and stay motivated, so it was good for me to be around demanding profs."

Q "I loved being able to take tutorials at Williams and **interact with professors and other students in very small groups**. This is a very good time for you to decide what you want to do after college, because some of the tutorial work is on the graduate level. If you are considering grad school, which many people are, or if you know that you want to be done with school after Williams, why not take these cool opportunities now to learn?"

Q "Upper-level classes at Williams get very intense, because that's where you begin to spend lots of time with your professors. You do have to get through some boring introductory classes first. Most **professors will be very welcoming and helpful** in their office hours, even if you are one of 50 students in the class. It gets much better in 200 and 300 levels, when class size decreases to 10 or so. You have to realize that you should be the one taking the initiative to meet your professors and do extra work."

Q "Majoring in political science at Williams has been great. Professors helped me identify career goals, find internships, and **go beyond coursework into real life**. Most classes I have taken in other departments have also been pretty good. I know that sometimes, if you really like your major, you focus primarily on classes in that department, but I took some really good history classes, some art, and a fair amount of English. I think that these were all somehow related to my interest in politics, so I just obtained a richer perspective."

Q "It's cool that classes at Williams are so small, but sometimes, professors pick on you in class, and that's intimidating. I think many people at Williams expect us to be super-confident and ready to be in college. The truth is, **when you come in as a freshman, you are just a kid**, and many other students can be arrogant and stifling."

Q "Williams encourages students to take classes in different areas. I came in wanting to do pre-med, and I switched to a double major in history and psychology instead. **Faculty members from all of those areas supported me in my decision**. I'm really glad they were so flexible and understanding. I think some people in my class have changed their majors three times by junior year, which tells you how much freedom you have to be learning and making smart choices."

Q "The English professors at Williams are truly inspiring. I think I chose it as a major because I just really enjoyed their company. Don't forget, though, that they hardly ever give out As, unless they find you attractive—just kidding. **English profs are quirky and intriguing**, but they know their limits, and so should you."

Q "Sometimes, I thought that the science professors I worked with were too interested in their own research careers to even notice students. However, there were enough of them who took the time to help me out when I needed it. Anthropology is not exactly the most popular major here, so you don't hear much about the resources the school has to offer. In actuality, **there is an abundance of resources**, as well as support and encouragement for those conducting their own research."

Q "I really liked the professors at Williams, but I think they **tolerate the jocks in the college and don't allow for a more intellectual climate**. Some people come to class in their gym clothes, chewing PowerBars and not bothering to do the reading or contribute to class. That attitude is really unfair and disrespectful to those of us who work hard, including the professors and teaching assistants who prepare for those classes."

Q "It's a pity that so few students at Williams major in Russian, because the department is absolutely awesome. I also took Japanese, but then I dropped it, because the professors were too strict and not at all encouraging. I also know that **most art professors are pretty cool**. I think after freshman year, you figure those things out and learn where to go for good advice and interesting classes."

Q "Many students think that it's next to impossible to get an A at Williams. I can tell you that if you spend enough time talking to your teachers, visiting their office hours, working on papers a little earlier than the day before the deadline, and just showing interest in what you are learning, you can get there. The A is worth it, but **the experience of earning it makes it great**. Then again, if you just want to go to college for sports and drinking, that's okay, too. Williams really doesn't pressure people that much to be very academic, but it doesn't cut anyone slack, either. You want to be a B student? Go ahead. You want an A? Well, do the work."

Q "As a student at Williams, I spent more time with my coaches than with my profs, because I was on two varsity teams. But the **professors never thought less of me** for not being a very academic person."

Q "I feel like some of the professors were too demanding and assigned **more homework than a normal person could handle**. I am pretty hardworking, but I think it is wrong to deprive yourself of sleep all the time. I know many kids develop stress-related psych disorders because of trying to cope with all of the work, and stay on top while not sleeping, eating, or socializing with friends. I think the school should try to make sure people stay healthy, even though they are the ones who choose to work so hard. Maybe they just need to be told to relax."

Q "It's very important to meet with your professors, go to their office hours, and just spend more time with them outside of class. They are really, really helpful, and they will let you **learn in the format that you feel most comfortable learning**."

Q "The professors are great, and it is really worth it to take more challenging classes with some of them—even if your grade is not as good as you expected. **Williams is not a place where you should shy away from things** you have not tried before. And the professors make those new things all the more appealing and accessible."

Q "I have **more than one favorite professor at Williams**, which says a lot. I think that being at Williams and learning from my professors has made me more mature."

The College Prowler Take On...
Academics

True, you have to work hard at Williams, and As are hard to get. However, the amount of personal attention and the quality of instruction make every bead of sweat worth it. Williams professors are accessible, articulate, and extremely erudite. Whatever their specific field, they share a commitment to encourage students to explore and learn, both within and beyond the classroom. Williams professors are also willing to devote whatever time necessary to help a student learn.

While the workload does vary with separate departments, students are constantly challenged to improve their skills and obtain new ones as well. They are also encouraged to share these achievements with others. Professors allow for each student to have his or her own style of learning, and they are supportive of everyone's individual learning process. Students have to work hard, but they enjoy help and inspiration from their professors every step of the way.

The College Prowler® Grade on
Academics: A

A high Academics grade generally indicates that professors are knowledgeable, accessible, and genuinely interested in their students' welfare. Other determining factors include class size, how well professors communicate, and whether or not classes are engaging.

Local Atmosphere

The Lowdown On...
Local Atmosphere

Region:
Northeast

City, State:
Williamstown, MA

Setting:
Berkshire Mountains

Distance from Boston:
Almost 3 hours

Distance from New York:
3.5 hours

Points of Interest:
Clark Art Institute Museum
MASS MoCA
North Adams
Williamstown

Closest Shopping Malls or Plazas:

Berkshire Mall

Colonial Plaza

North Adams Plaza

Closest Movie Theaters:

Images Cinema
50 Spring Street
Williamstown
(413) 458-5612

(Movie Theaters, continued)

North Adams Cinema 8
1665 Curran Highway
North Adams
(413) 663-5873

Regal Berkshire Mall 10
123 Old State Road at Route 8
Lanesboro
(413) 499-3106

Major Sports Teams:

Bruins (hockey)

Celtics (basketball)

Red Sox (baseball)

City Web Sites

www.williamstown.net

www.wtfestival.org

Did You Know?

5 Fun Facts about Williamstown:

- Williamstown was **established as a plantation** called West Hoosuck in 1753.
- The town has **more churches than bars**.
- The **Iranian royal family** was exiled in Williamstown in the 1970s.
- Williamstown celebrated it's **Ducentquinquagentennial** (250th birthday) on Saturday, September 20, 2003.
- The **Williamstown police** has two cars in total.

Famous People from Williamstown:

Susan B. Anthony – Born in Adams, Massachusetts, 10 miles from Williamstown.

Students Speak Out On...
Local Atmosphere

"Williamstown is so calm and peaceful. It's beautiful during all seasons. The town is small, but if you like the outdoors, you will really enjoy it."

Q "The town is composed almost entirely of college students, faculty, and other people related to Williams. So, while **you won't meet any cool town people**, you will always be surrounded by people who know how you're feeling."

Q "People in town are white, rich, and generally uninteresting. They **won't get in your way at all**, but if you are looking for fun beyond the school, get on the bus to New York."

Q "Williamstown has a **very welcoming atmosphere**. The Clark Art Museum attracts many visitors for a small town. Williamstown is really full of people from all over the place."

Q "The local atmosphere is similar to what you see in any random town in Massachusetts. It's quiet, white, and clean. **Churches are beautiful; the bars suck**. There are some really good restaurants—ridiculously expensive, but worth the time and money."

Q "Locals in Billsville are really friendly, from the post office staff to the random passerby. You get an overall sense of well-being and tranquility. There is a danger, however, that in four years, you will end up totally sedated and incapable of dealing with the real world. For example, you **get used to cars stopping before you cross the street**. Not a good habit to have in most other places in the world, especially big cities."

Q "The college and town buildings are gorgeous; the lawns are so well-kept. **What you see in those college catalogs is not enough** to show the beauty of Williamstown. In the fall, when the leaves change color, it gets prettier than those pictures."

Q "I don't know how to describe the local atmosphere, because there is no atmosphere. Nothing ever happens in the town except for college-related events. If you come from NYC, like myself, **you might end up really bored**. Breathing the clean air of the Berkshires is not enough sometimes, unless you spend most of your time in the library working."

Q "The College museum, the Clark, and MASS MoCA create the best atmosphere for those who wish to be immersed in the coffee shop. They are cozy and **serve some of the best cappuccinos in town**."

Q "It's funny that Williamstown is so small, and yet, **you meet all sorts of weird people**. There's one movie theater that shows weird and artsy movies, which is good if you are surrounded by perpetually drunken college jocks."

Q "Williamstown has a friendly, welcoming, and relaxing feel. Even when you stress about work, a walk in the **Hopkins Forest can lift your spirits**. Nobody will intrude on your privacy, ever; it's really nice."

Q "The town is kind of dead, in terms of social events—so don't rely on locals for having an actual social life. It's beautiful, but there's nothing special about it, except the fact that **there's a church on every corner**."

Q "I like walking around campus when I am stressed, bored, or just want to procrastinate. I've found that **there are more things to do than it seems**, and the overall atmosphere is very calm and nurturing."

Q "**Locals are friendly to college students** most of the time, and the atmosphere is just very cool and relaxing with the mountains always visible in the background."

Q "This is **one of the friendliest places you can go**, in addition to being one of the cleanest and the greenest. So enjoy it while you can."

Q "People might say that Williamstown is very small and not at all special, but I like the architecture and the cool museums. The **streets are also very clean and colorful**."

Q "Williamstown might be small, but it has a lot to offer in terms of scenery and events for the lovers of the arts. Most importantly, **you are always surrounded by people you can relate to**, even if you don't become the best of friends."

The College Prowler Take On...
Local Atmosphere

Williams is not comparable to New York City in the field of diversity, but for a small town, Williamstown has a lot to offer both visitors and residents. A friendly, inviting, and intellectually stimulating atmosphere, combined with peace and the beauty of nature, makes Williamstown more than attractive.

The town is small, but if you are into the arts, it has a lot to offer. From the movie theater to the overall appearance of the town, Williamstown gives off an artsy aura. Though it is generally quiet, many students find it relaxing.

The College Prowler® Grade on

Local Atmosphere: C+

A high Local Atmosphere grade indicates that the area surrounding campus is safe and scenic. Other factors include nearby attractions, proximity to other schools, and the town's attitude toward students.

Safety & Security

The Lowdown On...
Safety & Security

Number of WC Safety Officers:

11

WC Campus Safety:

Located in the basement of Hopkins Hall

Hours: Monday–Friday
8:30 a.m.–4:30 p.m.

(413) 597-4343

24-hours (non-emergencies):
(413) 597-4444

Emergencies: 911
(on campus, dial 9-911)

Safety Services:

24-hour patrols

Emergency phones

Escort service

Rape Agression Defense

Security alerts

Health Center:

Thompson Health Center

105 The Knolls

(413) 597-2206

Ext. 4567 for on-call physician

Hours: Monday–Friday
8:30 a.m.–9 p.m.,
Saturday–Sunday
1 p.m.–8 p.m.

Health Center Services:

Allergies

Clinics

Eating disorder treatment

Gynecology
(by appointment only)

HIV testing
(free and by appointment)

Immunizations

Laboratory

Peer health

Pharmacy

Psychological counseling

Sexual assault response team

Student health advisory

Rape and sexual assault hotline

Students Speak Out On...
Safety & Security

{ **"The campus looks safe, but sometimes, things go on at parties that should never happen and that most people don't report. I think some more female security officers would be good for this campus."**

Q "The security officers are very nice. They help people a lot, and I really like that **they offer to take you to your dorm after midnight**—not that Williamstown isn't a safe place in general. It just is comforting to know that they would do that."

Q "After 7 p.m. at Williams, random doors are locked for random purposes. This means people can't hand in papers and such. It's kind of ridiculous and annoying. The school hires **way too many people to do stupid bureaucratic stuff** like that, and our tuition money is spent on inane things like paying someone to lock a building that shouldn't be locked."

Q "Williams is a place where **your personal safety is a priority of the staff** and administration. My campus job was with the security office, and I loved it. They really try to take care of the students, and they listen to whatever suggestions you have for improvement. There is no reason to shy away from talking to a security officer when you need help. That's why they are here, and they like students a lot."

Q "As a first-year student at Williams, **I felt that everyone was concerned with my security** and tried to educate me about it. It wasn't just helpful, but what mattered most was that people cared."

Q "The college is obsessed with security. **When the stairs to Hopkins Hall get a little icy, they close them off** so nobody slips and falls. It's annoying, because then you have to walk all around the building in the snow to get to class."

Q "Everything is great at Williams, except the fact that if the health center is closed, then security has to drive you to the hospital. I just feel it's not their job to do that, because **they are not doctors**. The people who can't afford to call an ambulance have to rely on unprofessional people. One of my friends lost consciousness in class, and she refused to be taken care of because she knew her insurance could not cover it. This is ridiculous. It's not her fault that she passed out at a time when the health center was closed."

Q "I took a class called Rape Aggression Defense (RAD), taught by two of the best security officers and the kindest people on campus. **I learned a lot, and I'm happy I met those people**, because most of us kind of take them for granted as the guys in yellow jackets who walk around campus. They are actually responsible for many things we like about this place, safety being one."

Q "In the beginning of each school year, Williams organizes this huge talk on date rape. They don't teach you how to prevent it or anything, you just have to listen to this woman tell her experience. **I'm not sure that's helpful**, and why would someone want to tell their rape story in front of 400 people? It's also not fair that the presentation is mandatory for the frosh class to attend. Maybe we don't want to hear about it, either."

Q "Williamstown is a small town, and it's safe. The most you can do about your personal security is **make sure none of the other people in your dorm steal your shampoo** in the bathroom, which they will anyway."

Q "The Williams security officers have helped me out with so many things, from escorting me to my dorm at night to adjusting the heating in my dorm, even to waiting for me to finish my paper before they close up the language lab. It's nice to know that they are not just officers, **but have a very human side to them, too.**"

Q "**Security is a priority of the college,** but I feel that a lot more could be done, especially at weekend parties, which are always too crowded and nobody really checks who's 21 and stuff."

Q "I like that Williams security officers show respect and care for the students at all times. Some security measures are annoying and obsolete, like **locking up the door of a building where we all have to hand in our papers.** They know that many students need to get through one of the many doors of the building, yet lock all of them up; it's almost like they are doing it on purpose. What's even more ridiculous is at the same time, pretty much anyone can get into many other buildings that are no less important."

Q "Ah, security! Just when you think you are free to enjoy your life, there is some weird security regulation that gets in your way, like fire alarms that go off because someone is cooking Mexican food downstairs. I keep wondering why we have kitchens in the dorms, when every time someone uses them, the alarm goes off. Also, many **students now disregard the alarms,** which most of the time are not signaling a real problem. This is scary; when something does happen, will people take the alarm seriously enough not to burn alive?"

The College Prowler Take On...
Safety & Security

There is no doubt that the town and college of Williams are safe. Williams security tries to make it safer by locking random doors and making fire alarms sensitive to the smell of fried onions. At the same time, the health center is closed on weekends, when most college campus accidents occur, such as drinking problems and date rape.

The security staff are some of the friendliest and most caring people around, but their security priorities don't always make sense. Overall, the security staff makes sure the campus is safe and that students have a reliable source for their safety needs. Known for their prompt and kind help, security officers on campus could ease off closing the libraries and be more attentive to drinking problems, but all-in-all, they do a good job of making one feel safe at his or her home away from home.

A-

The College Prowler® Grade on

Safety & Security: A-

A high grade in Safety & Security means that students generally feel safe, campus police are visible, blue-light phones and escort services are readily available, and safety precautions are not overly necessary.

Computers

The Lowdown On...
Computers

High-Speed Network?
Yes

Wireless Network?
Yes

Number of Labs:
15

Number of Computers:
377

Operating Systems:
Windows, Mac OS X

24-Hour Labs:
Clark 201
Jesup 204
Kellogg Matt Cole Library

Free Software

Tons! Visit *http://oit.williams.edu/oit/software/index.cfm* for a complete list.

Discounted Software

Not from Williams, but get up to 85 percent off with a student discount on software from JourneyEd.com. Visit *www.efollett.com* for more information.

Charge to Print?

None

Did You Know?

Williams students get **daily e-mails** from the network manager, but no one has ever seen him.

Students Speak Out On...
Computers

"We have nice computers on campus, and I'm glad the school bought Macs, too, so whatever you want to use, you're all set."

Q "Williams has enough computers for those who didn't bring their own. It is thought by most that it is good to have a laptop on campus. **Don't trust any of the people that get paid by Williams** to connect your laptop to the school network, or to fix it. These people are likely to mess up big time."

Q "Computers are fine, even though if they crash, the staff is usually as clueless as you are. Printers are the real issue. The main computer building is equipped with about ten of them, and **not one works**. They are either out of paper, sleeping, broken, jammed, or someone spilled Mountain Dew on them."

Q "Computer labs are never crammed, and the Internet access is really fast. **There's a really cool media lab** for people who are into digital photography or film editing. If you meet the people who can help you use all the fancy technology, you are blessed."

Q "The Williams computer network is run by idiots. The **network is down every other day**, people lose papers, and they can't tell if their e-mails got delivered. Every couple of months, your e-mail account is not accessible, because you have to change your password. It sucks if this happens to be the day when you have a job application to mail."

Q "The labs aren't crowded, and generally, you can do your work. E-mail might be a problem, because **there's always something wrong with the *williams.edu* server**. Keep your Yahoo and Hotmail accounts activated."

Q "**Computers work better here than at other places** I have considered going to school. Signing up for classes online and being able to see your grades even when you are not on campus can be very useful. You have lots of space in your folder on the school server for keeping papers and downloading things."

Q "One time, my computer froze, and I brought it to the people in Jesup. They are supposed to be the ones who know about computers. Well, **they totally screwed up whatever was left functioning in my laptop**. I lost a 20-page paper, which I had saved both on the server and on the desktop. Then, they wanted to make me pay for re-installing some of my stuff. To make it even worse, one of them lost my power adaptor."

Q "Like most things in Williams, computers work. **You will feel spoiled when you leave**."

Q "Computers function at Williams, and **tons of coursework is done online**, posted, and e-mailed to professors. It saves a lot of time, and it keeps people informed about everything. Most of us check our e-mails at least every hour to stay on top of schoolwork and extracurricular commitments, and it works."

Q "The Internet access is fast when it is working, but lately we have had so many server problems, **I can no longer tell what is going on**."

Q "We have some great computer facilities, and **there is no reason for people to complain about anything**. The lousy setup of the Williams e-mail, which can be really annoying for attachments and paper submissions, is the only real complaint."

Q "Williams e-mail problems have done harm to many people's projects, and I feel that I can say that on behalf of the professors, too. There should be a way for e-mail to work normally, but **the current staff has no clue** about it, it seems."

Q "When **the network falls apart five times a day**, it's hard to make any polite comments."

Q "In the past, it has been terrible for everyone who deals with computers, which is, of course, the entire campus. **The power shutdown in the middle of finals was the straw that broke the camel's back** for me, because I almost lost my exam."

28 | COMPUTERS

www.collegeprowler.com

The College Prowler Take On...
Computers

C++ and other programming languages often seem to be the only languages that the Williams tech staff speaks. No one has been able to explain the daily network failures to us in actual English, so we can't say whose fault it is. Then again, the lost papers, job applications, and messages will never be retrieved, so why should we even feel the need to know the reason for the failures?

Williams computer facilities are truly wonderful, but with a network that falls apart every day, students cannot make full use of them. Students also feel that the tech staff is lacking in knowledge of how to fix common problems. It could be time for some lay-offs.

The College Prowler® Grade on
Computers: C+

A high grade in Computers designates that computer labs are available, the computer network is easily accessible, and the campus' computing technology is up-to-date.

Facilities

The Lowdown On...
Facilities

Student Center:
Goodrich Hall

Athletic Center:
Chandler Athletic Center

Libraries:
1914 Library
Archives and Special
Collections Library
Chapin Library of Rare Books
Matt Cole Library
Sawyer Library
Schow Science Library

Campus Size:
450 acres

Popular Places to Chill:
Baxter Snack Bar
Goodrich Coffee Bar
The Log

What Is There to Do on Campus?

Hang out at the Snack Bar, watch a free movie in Bronfman auditorium, drive up for dance parties in MASS MoCA, or go to a party.

Movie Theater on Campus?

No

Bowling on Campus?

No

Bar on Campus?

Yes, the Log

Coffeehouse on Campus?

Eco Café in Schow Library, Goodrich Coffee Bar

Favorite Things to Do

Chill in the Snack Bar

Play squash

Swim in the pool between 5 and 7 p.m.

Walk in Hopkins Forest

Did You Know?

The Williams College **libraries hold over 800,000 volumes**, and as a member of the Boston Library Consortium, have access to borrowing more than 20 million volumes from other libraries.

Students Speak Out On...
Facilities

"The observatory is one of the most precious facilities at Williams. It's a space where you can learn a lot and admire the skies to the fullest."

Q "The athletic facilities are amazing, from the pool to the squash center to the indoor track and also the dance studio. Another strength of Williams is the labs and other science facilities that are always available to all, and they are **staffed by some of the friendliest people ever**."

Q "Williams has truly amazing facilities. **Whatever they don't have, they build**, such as the new theater. The old theater was fine, too, with its various stage and rehearsal spaces. But now, it's even better."

Q "Libraries are very important facilities for me. At Williams, I have always thought that **looking for books and being in the library could never be more pleasant**. Schow library, in particular, catches the attention, with its modern shapes, high ceilings, and really, really good reading lights. Oh, I will miss the Schow lights when I leave."

Q "As a hockey player, I have to say that **our skating rink kicks butt**. I wish we had a bigger gym, though, because now, you have very busy times of the day when half the school wants to work out."

Q "Psych lab facilities and equipment are rarely mentioned in college catalogues, but for the sake of psych majors, I will say that they are great. **No wonder psych is one of the most popular Williams majors**."

Q "Sports facilities at Williams really couldn't be much better. Even **the outdoors fields are so well-maintained** that other schools can't compare."

Q "Art facilities at Williams are **very inviting and cozy**, since few people use them, anyways. I love the ceramics studio and the Spencer Art Building. If you want to do ceramics, there are actual potter wheels and a very good kiln."

Q **"**Any facility at Williams is very **modern, clean, and well-kept**. The school really puts a lot of money into this."

Q "The radio station has excellent equipment. **If you want to be a DJ, go for it**. And music facilities in general are very good."

Q "There's any facility you might need at Williams, from **a climbing wall to a farm nearby where you can take horseback riding lessons**. There is also a great lab for language learners and an office where you can borrow digital cameras, plus a lab where you can edit and improve digital photography and videos."

Q "Everyone knows that the College puts lots of money and effort into our sports facilities, and to me, this is clearly worth it, because the teams keep winning. Maybe they would win anyways, but **talented people deserve to enjoy good facilities**."

Q "I haven't thought much about Williams facilities, which is probably because **I take them for granted**. I have to wake up at six for bio labs, so I don't think much about how well Williams labs are equipped, and they are. So I am glad you asked me this question to begin with."

Q "I majored in psychology, which is not a major that requires as many facilities as other majors like biology, but it definitely requires more than history or math. Williams has **a really great lab for psych experience**, and if you design an experiment of your own, you will be provided with absolutely everything you might require."

Q "I didn't know until very recently that you could **borrow a digital camera from the school** and just play around, and then there's a separate lab where you can edit what you did. It's really cool."

Q "Theater facilities at Williams are top-notch. Some people actually think Williams doesn't need that much space for 20 theater majors per class, but I think **the theater facilities serve the summer theater festival**, and this brings a lot of people to see how nice our school is."

Q "Williams does not have a dance major, but **the dance facilities are really good**, and there is a variety of stuff you can try, from Irish to African dance and drumming to modern dance. I am happy with how they set up our performing space, because now that we get many people for our shows, I know that it matters which way people's seats would face, and how you position your dancers with the lighting, and the rest of the conditions you have."

Q "Yes, the facilities are excellent at Williams, which is partly why I did end up studying music after all. **I just couldn't miss out on the great opportunities** I would never have with music and recording in my home country. I know that Williams tries super-hard to give students a chance like this in other areas, but in music, I know from experience that it is amazing."

The College Prowler Take On...
Facilities

Want to have a special facility for basket-weaving and knot-tying? Just ask. Williams will provide the space, the equipment, and the materials at once. Luckily, most Williams facilities support activities that are much more meaningful than the ones aforementioned.

While many do argue that the quality of theater productions does not match the quality of the facility Williams built for theater and dance, it is reasonable to say that Williams students achieve good, if not excellent, results in many areas, including theater. The comfort of a well-designed and maintained facility helps people become better at what they do, whether it is playing the flute or kickboxing.

The College Prowler® Grade on

Facilities: A-

A high Facilities grade indicates that the campus is aesthetically pleasing and well-maintained; facilities are state-of-the-art, and libraries are exceptional. Other determining factors include the quality of both athletic and student centers and an abundance of things to do on campus.

Campus Dining

The Lowdown On...
Campus Dining

Freshman Meal Plan Requirement?
No

Meal Plan Average Cost:
$3,880

Places to Grab a Bite with Your Meal Plan:
Each dining hall offers the same menu during the week. For a list of what's available each day, go to *www.williams. edu/admin/dining/menu.php*.

Dodd Dining Hall
Food: Dining hall variety

Location: Dodd House

Hours: Monday–Thursday 7:30 a.m.–10 a.m., 11:30 a.m.–2 p.m., 5 p.m.–7:30 p.m., Sunday 11 a.m.–1 p.m., 5 p.m.–7:30 p.m.

Driscol Dining Hall
Food: Dining hall variety

Location: Driscol

Hours: Monday–Saturday 7:30 a.m.–10 a.m., 11:30 a.m.–2 p.m., 5 p.m.–7:30 p.m.,

(Driscol Dining Hall, continued)

Sunday 8 a.m.–9:30 a.m.,
11 a.m.–1 p.m.,
5 p.m.–7:30 p.m.

The Eco Café

Food: Organic fair trade coffee
and tea, cookies and biscotti
from local bakeries

Location: Science
building atrium

Hours: Monday–Friday
7:30 a.m.–3:30 p.m.

Grab 'n' Go

Food: Gourmet sandwiches,
fresh and bagged snacks

Location: Goodrich

Hours: Monday–Friday
10 a.m.–1 p.m.

Greylock

Food: Dining hall variety

Location: Greylock

Hours: Monday–Saturday
7:30 a.m.–10 a.m.,
11:30 a.m.–2 p.m.,
5 p.m.–8 p.m.,
Sunday 11 a.m.–1 p.m.,
5 p.m.–8 p.m.

Mission Park

Food: Dining hall variety

Location: Mission Park

Hours: Monday–Saturday
7:30 a.m.–10 a.m.,
11:30 a.m.–1:30 p.m.,
5 p.m.-7:30 p.m.,

(Mission Park, continued)

Sunday 8 a.m.–9:30 a.m.,
11 a.m.–1 p.m.,
5 p.m.–7:30 p.m.

Snack Bar

Food: Bake-shop, sandwiches,
sundaes, pizza

Location: Mission Park

Hours: Sunday–Wednesday
8:30 p.m.–12:30 a.m.,
Thursday–Friday
8:30 p.m.–2 a.m.,
Saturday 8:30 p.m.–3 a.m.

Off-Campus Places to Use Your Meal Plan:

The Log

Food: Snack food in a
pub atmosphere

Location: Spring Street

Hours: Tuesday–Wednesday
8 p.m.–12 a.m., Thursday–
Friday 8 p.m.–1 a.m.

Student Favorites:

Brunch Night at Greylock
Tuesday and Thursday nights

24-Hour On-Campus Eating?

No

Students Speak Out On...
Campus Dining

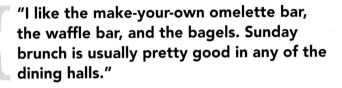

"I like the make-your-own omelette bar, the waffle bar, and the bagels. Sunday brunch is usually pretty good in any of the dining halls."

Q "We have Grab 'n' Go, which is really neat, because it lets you make your own bag lunch when you are in a rush to get to class. **Grab 'n' Go has gotten so much better these days**, with the salads they offer and the brownies."

Q "Food in Williams is generally good. I think sometimes they just make food for too many people, so **they mess up or run out of things**. We have the annual lobster dinner, though, which rocks."

Q "I love on-campus food, and the fact that **you can come back for as many helpings as you wish**. The only thing is, they can't cook fish properly, and they serve these bland, boiled fish dishes sometimes, but the meat is pretty good, especially fried chicken in all of its varieties."

Q "The dining hall and the Snack Bar staff are the friendliest people on campus and anywhere else. **They put so much effort into everything, and it works**, from international food nights to stress busters during exam week."

Q "**I have no complaints about the food**, but I wonder who washes the dishes because I keep finding greasy spots on them."

Q "I wish they cooked something different once in a while, like Chinese food. The rice in the dining hall is the kind you can throw at a wall, and it would stick there. **The desserts are always really yummy**, though, especially the ice cream: Oreo, cookie dough, and mint chocolate chip ice cream. There are also the famous ski team bars, named after the ski team, but nobody knows why."

Q "The **food is fine**, but the selection of coffee and tea sucks, and the juice machines are always malfunctioning. The soda machines work just fine, but who wants Diet Coke three times a day?"

Q "Dining on campus should be open all the time, not just between the hours of 5 p.m. and 7 p.m., because some of us have stuff to do then, and **if you miss dinner, you wait on a long line to get your dinner points** or just spend extra money on food."

Q "Goodrich Coffee Bar. **If you have an early class, this is the way to go**. Just walk into the room with your warm breakfast, and keep yourself awake through the 8:30 a.m. lecture."

Q "I don't eat in the dining hall too much because I prefer to buy organic food. **Most of their vegetables are not organic and have no actual flavor**. But I have to admit that they have good food options, and they serve fresh and warm stuff."

Q "**I used to really like the food** my freshman year, but then it got repetitive. Since then, I cook a lot. My dorm has a very nice kitchen, and we keep it more or less clean."

Q "I worked in the dining hall for some extra cash. Well, I can tell you from experience that **the people there try really hard to please everybody's taste** and help out students with special needs. I also think the nutritional value of what we eat at Williams is pretty good."

Q "**Dining halls are generally okay, and they are very nice on some occasions**. I guide tours for the school, and the parents always like the way the dining is set up with the salad bar. I think some students might want dining hall hours to run a little later so they have more time after practice and such."

Q "The salad bar was never what I expected. I think the dining halls should **work on getting better and fresher veggies**."

Q "I really like that the **helpings are unlimited**. Some think this might be why so many people gain weight, but eventually, they tend to lose it and learn to eat healthy. The dining hall staff does very nice things, like taking family recipes from students and making them. And then their theme dinners are just awesome. They keep everything clean and in full supply, and they have good opening hours."

Q "During exam week, the dining halls on campus do late-night snacks. **It is just what everyone needs**."

The College Prowler Take On...
Campus Dining

While they may not make the best veggie pizza on earth, the campus dining facilities do an adequate job of allowing vegetarians and other individuals with diverse eating habits to stay satisfied. Most of the time, the food actually tastes good and is fresh.

Many agree that the fruit and vegetable portion of the menu could use some work, but it could be a lot worse. Williams on-campus dining has also been very successful in creating a pleasant atmosphere for enjoying your food, and they might surprise you with new recipes and touches.

The College Prowler® Grade on
Campus Dining: B

Our grade on Campus Dining addresses the quality of both school-owned dining halls and independent on-campus restaurants, as well as the price, availability, and variety of food.

Off-Campus Dining

The Lowdown On...
Off-Campus Dining

Restaurant Prowler:
Popular Places to Eat!

Chopsticks Restaurant
Food: Asian
412 Main Street
Williamstown
(413) 458-5750
Price: $8–$20 per person
Hours: Daily 10:30 a.m.–10:30 p.m.

Hobson's Choice
Food: American variety
159 Water Street
Williamstown
(413) 458-9101
Price: $12–$28 per person
Hours: Daily 5 p.m.–9:30 p.m.

Hot Tomatoes

Food: Pizza

100 Water Street
Williamstown

(413) 458-2722

Price: $8–$22 per person

Hours: Sunday–Saturday
7 a.m.–2 p.m., 4 p.m.–1 a.m.

Papa Charlie's

Food: Homemade food,
sandwiches

28 Spring Street
Williamstown

(413) 458-5969

Price: $8–$12 per person

Hours: Monday–Saturday
8 a.m.–8 p.m.,
Sunday 8 a.m.–7 p.m.

Red Herring

Food: Pub

46 Spring Street
Williamstown

(413) 458-2808

Price: $4–$12 per person

Hours: Daily 5 p.m.–10 p.m.,
Bar open until 1 a.m.

Spice Root

Food: Indian

23 Spring Street
Williamstown

(413) 458-5200

Price: $12–$20 per person

Hours: Monday–Saturday
11:30 a.m.–2:30 p.m.,
5 p.m.–10 p.m.,
Sunday 12 p.m.–3 p.m.,
5 p.m.–10 p.m.

Thai Garden

Food: Thai

27 Spring Street
Williamstown

(413) 458-0004

Price: $8–$20 per person

Hours: Daily
11:30 a.m.–10 p.m.

Yasmin's Restaurant

Food: American

The Orchards Hotel
222 Adams Road
Williamstown

(413) 458-9611

Price: $8–$32 per person

Hours: Daily
7 a.m.–10:15 a.m.,
12 p.m.–2:15 p.m.,
5 p.m.–9 p.m.

Student Favorites:

Chopsticks Restaurant

Hot Tomatoes

Papa Charlie's

Thai Garden

Closest Grocery Store:

Stop 'n Shop

876 State Road

North Adams

(413) 664-8100

Best Pizza:

Hot Tomatoes

Best Chinese:

Chopsticks Restaurant

Best Breakfast:

Papa Charlie's

Best Place to Take Your Parents:

Hobson's Choice

24-Hour Eating:

No

Other Places to Check Out:

Subway

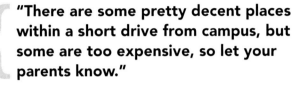

Students Speak Out On...
Off-Campus Dining

"There are some pretty decent places within a short drive from campus, but some are too expensive, so let your parents know."

Q "**Thank God for the Indian restaurant**, because the dining hall food has no spices at all."

Q "I love Thai food, and the Thai place in Williamstown just rules my world. **It's not too expensive either, and you can do takeout**."

Q "There aren't too many options for off-campus food, but the ones that we have are awesome. For a small town, **we've done great with the Indian, Thai, and Latin American places** next to each other and the Greek owners of the sandwich shop. Well, there's also Subway, I guess."

Q "I wish I didn't have to drive out of town for a good Chinese place, even though they deliver. Most **good restaurants are far from campus**, so when it's cold, snowing, or we have too much work, it's just not convenient."

Q "The bakery and the ice cream **shops on Spring Street are amazing**. I worked in one of them, and it was great."

Q "I miss good pizza a lot. Even the best Williamstown **pizza can't compare to what you can get in Chicago**. I wish we had more ethnic restaurants."

Q "The pub, **Red Herring, serves good burgers and cheap beer**. This works for me just fine."

Q "Yeah, you can eat out, but it's really expensive. I like the sandwich shop, Papa Charlie's, because **they have very original sandwiches and nice atmosphere**. Unfortunately, I can't eat there everyday."

Q "Go to Hobson's Choice if you drive around this area. It is worth it. Williamstown is small, but I feel like **it has at least one good restaurant**."

Q "Williamstown has nice restaurants, but they are not many, and **it sucks, because you always meet your classmates going on dates there**. It's embarrassing. You can't eat in privacy."

Q "You might never find a good hairdresser in this town, but at least there are good restaurants. **Nobody ever left a restaurant feeling sorry they went in**. It's different with the hairdresser."

Q "My friend works for a restaurant nearby, so I go there with other friends, and we are almost regulars now. It's a nice place, **not too fancy, but enough for a good dinner**."

Q "Spice Root (the Indian restaurant on Spring Street) is actually **pretty affordable, and their food is really good**. Maybe your Indian friends would say it could be better, but I love their lunch menus, especially the cabbage."

Q "Eating out is an important pastime around here, because **Williamstown doesn't really have good bars** and compensates with having really good restaurants that are very accessible."

Q "Watch out with off-campus dining, or you will become like me—totally addicted to the sandwich place on Spring Street. They have very original sandwiches and **awesome Greek salads and smoothies**. Just down the street is a great ice cream place. I have to say, after spending three years in this town, I haven't gotten tired of any of them."

Q "There are **many good restaurants in the area**, and some of my friends happen to have part-time jobs there, so we have tested those places inside and out, and they have great food."

The College Prowler Take On...
Off-Campus Dining

There could always be more variety in a small town. However, for its size, this town has a lot to offer when it comes to good food. It is true, though, that some of the restaurants are so expensive that you have to wait for your parents to come to visit and take you out.

But fear not, there are several that are still affordable. There are also a couple of all-time favorites that no one even tries to grade anymore; they are just known to offer great quality and are constantly frequented by Williams students.

The College Prowler® Grade on

Off-Campus Dining: C+

A high Off-Campus Dining grade implies that off-campus restaurants are affordable, accessible, and worth visiting. Other factors include the variety of cuisine and the availability of alternative options (vegetarian, vegan, Kosher, etc.).

Campus Housing

The Lowdown On...
Campus Housing

Room Types:
Singles, doubles, suite-style singles and doubles, co-ops

Best Dorms:
Dodd
Perry
Spencer

Worst Dorms:
Currier
Prospect

Undergrads Living on Campus:
93%

Number of Dorms:
41

Dormitories:

Agard
Floors: 3
Total Occupancy: 24
Bathrooms: Shared by floor
Coed: Yes
Residents: Upperclassmen
Room Types: Singles, doubles
Special Features: Huge rooms, parking, large lawn, laundry

Brooks House
Floors: 2 plus basement
Total Occupancy: 17
Bathrooms: Shared by two rooms
Coed: Yes
Residents: Upperclassmen
Room Types: Singles
Special Features: Laundry, parking, disability accomodations

Chadbourne House
Floors: 2
Total Occupancy: 14
Bathrooms: Shared by floor
Coed: Yes
Residents: Upperclassmen
Room Types: Singles, doubles
Special Features: Balcony

Currier House
Floors: 3
Total Occupancy: 62
Bathrooms: Shared by floor
Coed: Yes
Residents: Upperclassmen
Room Types: Singles, doubles
Special Features: Common room has piano, ballroom, kitchen, fireplaces

Dodd Annex
Floors: 2
Total Occupancy: 11
Bathrooms: Shared by floor
Coed: Yes
Residents: Upperclassmen
Room Types: Singles
Special Features: Front porch

Dodd House
Floors: 4
Total Occupancy: 58
Bathrooms: Shared by room
Coed: Yes
Residents: Upperclassmen
Room Types: Singles, doubles
Special Features: Laundry, parking, restaurant, party room

Doughty House

Floors: 3

Total Occupancy: 11

Bathrooms: Shared by floor

Coed: Yes

Residents: Upperclassmen

Room Types: Singles

Special Features: Eat-in kitchen and living room

East College

Floors: 3

Total Occupancy: 64

Bathrooms: Shared by floor

Coed: Yes

Residents: Freshmen

Room Types: Singles, doubles

Special Features: Laundry, common lounges

Fayerweather Hall

Floors: 3

Bathrooms: Shared by floor

Coed: Yes

Residents: Freshmen

Room Types: Singles, doubles

Special Features: Laundry, common lounges

Fitch House

Floors: 3

Total Occupancy: 44

Bathrooms: Shared by floor

Coed: Yes

Residents: Upperclassmen

Room Types: Singles, doubles

Special Features: Common rooms, kitchen, rec room

Garfield House

Floors: 3

Total Occupancy: 36

Bathrooms: Shared by floor

Coed: Yes

Residents: Upperclassmen

Room Types: Singles, doubles

Special Features: Living room, library, large lawn

Goodrich House

Floors: 3

Total Occupancy: 10

Bathrooms: Shared by floor

Coed: Yes

Residents: Upperclassmen

Room Types: Singles, 1 double

Special Features: Kitchen, dining room, front porch, disability accessible

Greylock Quad (Bryant, Mark Hopkins, Gladden, and Carter)

Floors: 4 in each building

Total Occupancy: 297

Bathrooms: Shared by floor

Coed: Yes

Residents: Upperclassmen

Room Types: Singles, doubles

Special Features: Laundry, kitchen, large windows

Lambert House

Floors: 2

Total Occupancy: 8

Bathrooms: Shared by floor

Coed: Yes

Residents: Upperclassmen

Room Types: Singles

Special Features: Living room, front porch, kitchen, laundry

Lehman Hall

Floors: 3

Bathrooms: Shared by floor

Coed: Yes

Residents: Freshmen

Room Types: Singles, doubles

Special Features: Disability accommodations, laundry, TV lounge

Mary Hubbell House

Floors: 3

Total Occupancy: 27

Bathrooms: Shared by room

Coed: Yes

Residents: Upperclassmen

Room Types: Singles, doubles

Special Features: Kitchen, bay windows, front porch

Mission Park (Armstrong, Dennett, Mills, and Pratt)

Floors: 5 in each building

Total Occupancy: 294

Bathrooms: Shared by floor

Coed: Yes

Residents: Sophomores

Room Types: Singles

Special Features: Has its own dining hall, common rooms

Morgan Hall

Floors: 4

Bathrooms: Shared by floor or suite

Coed: Yes

Residents: Freshmen

Room Types: Suite-style, singles, doubles

Special Features: Disability accommodations, laundry facility

Perry House

Floors: 3

Total Occupancy: 25

Bathrooms: Shared by floor

Coed: Yes

Residents: Upperclassmen

Room Types: Singles, doubles

Special Features: Goat room, laundry, kitchen

Prospect House

Floors: 5

Total Occupancy:

Bathrooms: Shared by floor

Coed: Yes

Residents: Upperclassmen

Room Types: Singles, doubles, suite-style

Special Features: Common rooms, laundry

Sage Hall

Floors: 4

Bathrooms: Shared by floor

Coed: Yes

Residents: Freshmen

Room Types: Singles, doubles, some arranged in mini-suites

Special Features: Disability accommodations, laundry, common rooms for suite-style doubles and singles

Spencer House

Floors: 3

Total Occupancy: 24

Bathrooms: Shared by floor

Coed: Yes

Residents: Upperclassmen

Room Types: Singles, doubles

Special Features: Laundry, kitchen

Thompson House

Floors: 3

Total Occupancy: 30

Bathrooms: Shared by floor

Coed: Yes

Residents: Upperclassmen

Room Types: Singles, doubles

Special Features: Close to Mission dining hall, kitchen, laundry

Tyler Annex

Floors: 2

Total Occupancy: 20

Bathrooms: Shared by floor

Coed: Yes

Residents: Mostly sophomores

Room Types: Singles

Special Features: Common rooms, laundry, kitchen

Tyler House

Floors: 3

Total Occupancy: 38

Bathrooms: Shared by floor

Coed: Yes

Residents: Upperclassmen

Room Types: Singles, doubles

Special Features: Large living rooms

West College
Floors: 5
Total Occupancy: 50
Bathrooms: Shared by floor
Coed: Yes
Residents: Mostly seniors
Room Types: Singles, doubles
Special Features: Full kitchen, large living room, laundry

Williams Hall
Floors: 4
Bathrooms: Shared by room
Cosed: Yes
Residents: Freshmen
Room Types: Singles, doubles
Special Features: Disability accommodations, laundry, common rooms for suite-style doubles and singles

Woodbridge House
Floors: 3
Total Occupancy: 14
Bathrooms: Shared by floor
Coed: Yes
Residents: Upperclassmen
Room Types: Singles
Special Features: Kitchen, laundry

Wood House
Floors: 3
Total Occupancy: 27
Bathrooms: Shared by floor
Coed: Yes
Residents: Upperclassmen
Room Types: Singles, 1 double
Special Features: Common rooms, kitchen, laundry, parking

Housing Offered:
Singles: 82%
Doubles: 18%
Triples/Suites: 0%
Apartments: 0%

Bed Type
Extra-long twin

Cleaning Service?
Cleaning of floor bathrooms, garbage removal

You Get
Ethernet jacks, bed, desk, dresser

Also Available
Cable TV in common rooms

Students Speak Out On...
Campus Housing

{ **"Williams dorms have been getting better and better during my time in the school. Some of the less convenient places were renovated, especially sophomore dorms."**

Q "You have to choose your dorm carefully, because things are very different from place to place. The overall quality of housing is good, but in some dorms, **you have to share a bathroom with another five or six people**, maybe even more. Some do their laundry by hand, and you find their dirty socks in the sink. Others peel onions in the bathroom. And then others take an hour to shower. It's college life, but at Williams, you can avoid it if you pick the right dorm with the right people."

Q "**I had a mouse in my dorm once**, and the housing office put so much effort into getting rid of it that my roommate nearly got her foot into a trap they had set up for the mouse."

Q "In my dorm, there was always a line for the bathroom, but never for the laundry. I guess **one of the people in our dorm just took forever in the shower**. In most dorms, you would do just fine, though."

Q "Before you leave for any break, you have to take all of your stuff out of the bathroom. If you don't do it the second they want you to do it, **the custodial staff will throw all of your shampoo away**, or keep it for themselves—who knows."

Q "Williams College has a perverted custom called 'the housing lottery.' **It's supposed to be fair, but it is not**. If you are picking with upperclassmen, you could get a good number and pick whatever dorm you like, but if you are picking with people from your class, you are screwed."

Q "**If you have a car, there are some very nice dorms you could live in**. But if you don't want to walk in the cold, you might want to pick the ones that are close to buildings where classes meet. My own dorm was very close to the gym and to the arts building, where I spent lots of time painting."

Q "Most dorm rooms in Williams are very big and nice. **Common room spaces are available** in most dorms, and many have a TV in them. Many dorms also have nice kitchens if you are into cooking at all. I also appreciate the pool tables and the laundry machines."

Q "**I never had a roommate at Williams**, not even freshman year. I enjoyed the privacy very much. At the same time, I knew I could room with someone if I had wanted to, and living alone never made my social life any less fun."

Q "Some Williams dorms, and many buildings in general, have horrible heating systems. **You can't control the heat from your room**, and it's so strong that the air gets really dry. People get nosebleeds, eye problems, and live in a furnace."

Q "You can't rely on Williams housing to make a comfortable living situation. **You will buy your own chairs, blankets, pillows, and everything else** you might need to make a nice room."

Q "The rooms are nice, but the closet spaces can't fit all of my stuff. **I got a Williams carpenter to make me another one of those cabinets**, so I could actually put my clothes in it. That was very nice of them."

Q "Housing at Williams is good if you are American, but if you are an international student, it sucks. **You have the right of only two boxes of summer storage**, and I had to throw away things that I owned and had brought from home. It's really sad when you see other students loading tons of things in their pick-up trucks to know that a box of books that you brought from home has to go in the garbage."

Q "Williams' dorms are nice. **The wooden floors create a sense of warmth**, and some are even carpeted. Windows are big enough to let air in. Even from the outside, most dorms look cool."

Q "Dorms are nice, but the people who are responsible for assigning you to a room are horrible. **I had to spend an entire year in a dorm with carpeted floors**, which I am allergic to because of one of the materials they are made from. Nobody cared, even though I told them."

Q "It really sucks when your dorm is next to a construction site, and you can only enjoy the quiet in your room for about two hours a day. **I could never do homework in my own room**, or even just take a nap or relax— it sucked."

Q "**I hated the common bathroom**, because it had to accommodate way more people than it could, and it was hard to keep it clean."

Q "The lighting in most Williams rooms is really poor, so bring lamps from home. And **bring lots of patience for the people who are responsible for Williams buildings**. They never do things in time, and they are likely to mess up big time. When I lost my key, they came and changed the lock of the room next to mine, so they would get two people locked out instead of one."

The College Prowler Take On...
Campus Housing

Although some people do get lucky, most underclassmen are crammed into small rooms and bathrooms, and even some upperclassmen end up in a room where they have to hear a drilling noise for 10 hours a day. Relying on the buildings and grounds staff to help out with anything is not a good idea. They are notorius for creating plenty of red tape; they waste people's time more than anything else. Unlike any other office on campus, they are also known to be rude at times, and they're rumored to be fans of construction, jack-hammering and drilling at the early hours of the morning.

At the same time, though, construction and renovation have had very positive impacts on some dorms, while the overall comfort, hygiene, and accessibility have always been excellent. It just seems as if the positives and negatives balance each other out.

The College Prowler® Grade on
Campus Housing: C

A high Campus Housing grade indicates that dorms are clean, well-maintained, and spacious. Other determining factors include variety of dorms, proximity to classes, and social atmosphere.

Off-Campus Housing

The Lowdown On...
Off-Campus Housing

Undergrads in Off-Campus Housing:

7%

Best Time to Look for a Place:

Applications are due February 7. Begin looking before this date, but you do not have to have a place lined up to apply for off-campus housing.

Popular Areas:

Main Street, Water Street

For Assistance:

www.williams.edu/admin-depts/bg/housing

(413) 597-2195

E-mail: housing@williams.edu

Off-Campus Permission

Students must apply through Williams to live off campus. Housing is not guaranteed, and students may not sign a lease without receiving permission first. Only second-semester juniors, seniors, married students, and non-traditional students may live off campus. Permission is given to a limited number of students, and students living off campus will not be eligible for on-campus housing the following year.

Students Speak Out On...
Off-Campus Housing

"Few people live off campus because campus dorms are just fine. If you did live off campus, you would still be fairly close to the College, so it's not like you can isolate yourself."

Q "Why would you live off campus? **You lose the fast Internet connection**."

Q "**I gave up the thought of living off campus**, because my dining hall is in my dorm now, and I don't even need to go out in the cold to get food, do laundry, or play pool."

Q "**Williamstown is not that cheap**, and it might not be worth it to live off campus."

Q "I lived off campus last year, and it was nice to know that **I don't need my school ID to get into the building**. But paying bills, shopping, and having your own phone line set up is just too much trouble when you are also taking five classes at an academically-challenging school."

Q "Well, you will live off campus for the rest of your life, so **I just don't see what the advantages are** of doing it now."

Q "Living off campus can save you some money if you are **careful about where you shop and how much furniture you buy**. It will make your life harder in other random ways, like dealing with a cranky landlord and a neighbor who hates loud music."

Q "**Having your own bathroom is the only reason** to live off campus, but you might still have to share."

Q "**Living off campus is pointless** in a town as small as this. The school is the town. You will always be on campus, anyway."

Q "I kind of liked living off campus, but just for a semester, when the dorm I was assigned to turned out to be close to this construction ground. So I just avoided the noise, but then **I came back to the dorm living situation**. I guess the point is who you live with and whether you have enough room, but when you're in college, you don't need that much more. I mean, I am never in my room anyway, so why rent an entire house in town, or even a floor of a house?"

Q "I lived off campus for a year and was fine. The campus is small, so **I didn't feel left out or isolated**. I enjoyed more freedom of what I could do in my house, and I had no obnoxious neighbors like you would in a dorm."

Q "If you get together with a couple of friends to live off campus, you are in for a great experience, because then you are the ones who set the rules in your own house instead of depending on Williams staff and administration. Prices will vary with the location, but **you don't want to be too far away from class when it gets cold**."

Q "**No matter where you live, you will be in Williams**, because the College is the most important thing in town. So you might as well be in a dorm and do the whole college thing."

The College Prowler Take On...
Off-Campus Housing

Most students agree living off campus is not really an option. Because Williams is a small school, there is plenty of housing available on campus. Williamstown is a small town, and there are not many places to stay. The smallness of the town and the College makes living on campus the most logical option.

Some students choose to live off campus, though, and they value their experiences. Off-campus housing is generally near the campus, but costs of renting can be pretty high. Many students enjoy the freedom of living on their own and getting to set their own rules. The housing policy regarding off-campus housing is rather tough. The number of students permitted to live off campus is limited, as are the options.

The College Prowler® Grade on

Off-Campus Housing: C-

A high grade in Off-Campus Housing indicates that apartments are of high quality, close to campus, affordable, and easy to secure.

Diversity

The Lowdown On...
Diversity

Native American:
Less than 1%

White:
66%

Asian American:
9%

International:
6%

African American:
10%

Out-of-State:
84%

Hispanic:
8%

Political Activity

Liberal on campus are rampant, and students are in groups such as MassPIRG which are relatively active on campus.

Gay Pride

Gay pride is high, but in the past, some homophobic e-mails were sent out to the members of the Queer Student Union.

Most Popular Religions

The most popular faiths on campus are Protestantism and Catholicism.

Economic Status

The majority of students are wealthy and upper-middle-class.

Minority Clubs

Asian American Students in Action (AASiA), Black Student Union, Harrison Morgan Brown Pre-Medical Society, International Club, Jewish Student Union, Koreans of Williams, QSU, SASA, VISTA

Students Speak Out On...
Diversity

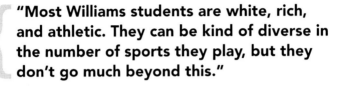

"Most Williams students are white, rich, and athletic. They can be kind of diverse in the number of sports they play, but they don't go much beyond this."

Q "I am one of not very many blacks on campus, and I know from my own experience that the place is not really diverse. **You end up hanging out with the same two or three people all the time**, and they are just like you."

Q "**Diversity is a state of mind**, not a number of people. In this sense, Williams is diverse, because all of the students have very open minds and are curious about other cultures. Here, you can meet people from all over America, and the world, if you take the time and make some effort."

Q "Williams is not the most diverse place, but there isn't pressure to be like the majority. **If you aren't a jock, you won't be popular**, but you will still have friends, and no one will look down on you ever."

Q "Williams is boring and preppy. **Few interesting people spice up the scene**, and you must find them as soon as you go to freshman orientation. If you wear polo shirts and J.Crew outfits, though, you will fit right in."

Q "This school is a production line for investment bankers. The student body is not diverse, and the companies who come to recruit are not either. **Don't be misled by the pictures of cute Hispanic girls** in the catalogue."

Q "We have some **pretty cool international students** from all over the world, especially from Jamaica."

Q "Williams is okay for a small school, because **every school has a type of student they look for**; we've got mostly jocks, but it doesn't mean that the school is not diverse."

Q "I think **the admissions office has made it their goal to admit the richest white kids in the States** and make them good, even better, athletes than they were when they applied. What do you mean, diversity?"

Q "My girlfriend is Turkish, and my best friend is from Kenya. **Diversity is important** in your personal life, and Williams gives you the opportunity to have it."

Q "I met some pretty cool people in my four years, **all from different majors and with different hobbies**, and so this helped me learn a lot about diversity."

Q "There are a handful of international students who always stick together and don't mix with the rest to of us. **Minority students also stay in their own little groups.** I don't know how you can have diversity."

Q "You can't have diversity in a place like this. They are committed mostly to educating rich white kids and **sending them to Wall Street**."

Q "Williams is not really diverse, but not completely uniform either. They are working on it. I think **we have many Asian students**, which is great, but too few blacks and Hispanics. In general, most people have very similar social backgrounds."

Q "Where is the diversity? **Look at everyone in his or her pink polo shirts and J.Crew sandals**. Nobody in their right mind can call this diversity."

The College Prowler Take On...
Diversity

To say that Williams tries hard to attract people from diverse backgrounds is just a euphemism for saying that Williams always ends up admitting people who belong to the same social group. Williams should not even try to argue that diversity is a top priority on the list of admissions officers.

Too many students have parents who attended the school for this to be true. But, if you are looking for diversity within a majority group of white, wealthy, preppy, and athletic people, you might find it.

The College Prowler® Grade on

Diversity: C

A high grade in Diversity indicates that ethnic minorities and international students have a notable presence on campus and that students of different economic backgrounds, religious beliefs, and sexual preferences are well-represented.

Guys & Girls

The Lowdown On...
Guys & Girls

Men Undergrads:	Women Undergrads:
49%	51%

Birth Control Available?

Yes, at the health center pharmacy, students can buy condoms, birth control pills, and the morning-after pill.

Social Scene

Everyone works very hard during the week and gets very, very drunk during weekends, so they can forget what happened and go back to their work on Sunday night. Many parties are run by athletic teams.

Hookups or Relationships?

Mostly hookups; relationships do happen, but most people are not looking for a long-term commitment.

Best Place to Meet Guys/Girls

Brooks Late-Night, a party on Saturday

Dress Code

Flip-flops, sweatpants, tank-tops, Williams T-shirts

Did You Know?

Top Three Places to Find Hotties:

1. Brooks
2. Perry
3. The gym

Top Four Places to Hook Up:

1. Perry Goat Room
2. Rooftop of Hopkins Observatory
3. Currier Ballroom
4. The football field

Students Speak Out On...
Guys & Girls

"Most guys are really hot, because they play sports and have gorgeous bodies, but they are not into committed relationships, which makes it hard if you are a girl and you don't go for one-night stands."

Q "Williams girls dress and act like guys. I don't know how they think someone can be attracted to them. **They look sloppy and don't take care of themselves**. Very few wear nice shoes, for example, or cool makeup, or try to look like they put forth some effort."

Q "Guys at Williams always hang out with a crowd of guys, so you can't talk to them. **It's like we're back in middle school**."

Q "**Williams girls care more about their grades** and the sports they play than about guys. Even the less hot ones."

Q "Guys at Williams are very immature. **They drink too much and can be obnoxious at parties**, trying to touch you. Many are good-looking, but it's not worth it."

Q "There are some pretty hot girls at Williams, **on the track and tennis team in particular**. They make you feel like you have a friend who can go running with you, climbing, throwing a Frisbee and stuff—not just going out for dinner all dressed up."

Q "**Williams guys treat girls like their buddies— it's so lame**. They think they can burp and fart while you're there and use bad words."

Q "Williams girls are cute and smart, but everyone has their little group of friends, and it's hard to meet other people and date. **Many people are too shy to even talk to each other**, and it's not like you can walk up to a girl in the dining hall and tell her you're attracted to her."

Q "**Williams guys make no effort to win a girl**. They think girls should be making steps, and this is totally wrong."

Q "If you are gay, there's going to be between **three and five hot guys on campus that are out as being gay** and available. At least two of them will not be your type of guy, and one will be too weird. The other two, hopefully, are into threesomes and will invite you to join."

Q "I think that **the number of really hot lesbian girls on campus has really increased**, and that many of them are serious about relationships, unlike straight girls who only hook up once in a while."

Q "**Williams guys are cute**, and they act respectfully to a girl most of the time, even in their drunken moments."

Q "Girls at Williams **don't make any effort to look good during weekdays**, so then you see them all dressed up at a party, and you can't even tell who they are. Strange stuff."

Q "**Williams girls are very work-driven**. Most of them act like they don't really need a guy at this stage."

Q "Williams guys must get better after they graduate, because throughout college, **they remain immature and so annoying**."

Q "A lot of **people are seeing someone who is not from the school**. That's nice, because the school is too small anyways, and there's no reason why you should just choose one of the people in your dorm or something. I don't know if it is fair to evaluate guys and girls on this campus because they are very different."

Q "I was not that interested in dating during my first year here, and **most of my friends were single**. Things changed later, but I am glad there was no pressure to date someone, and you could make your work a priority or just take your time to adjust to college."

Q "**The average Williams guy is not interested in a relationship** but would readily have sex with some random girl, as long as this does not interfere with his football practice the next day. Pure and simple."

Q "Williams girls are not known to be the most attractive, because they just don't try too hard to impress. As a guy, though, I like more than having a girl wear high heels and makeup. **Girls here look natural and sincere**. I like that."

Q "Long-lasting **friendships between people at Williams often result in marriages** after college, which is a scary thought to me, as I look at my friends now."

The College Prowler Take On...
Guys & Girls

Guys and girls at Williams and elsewhere spend a lot of time complaining about each other, but the truth is that they are just like most college students. Williams students are good-looking and athletic and like to have a lot of fun. Maturity might come to some of them well after college, but most create strong friendships, and those who wish to commit do form relationships.

It is said that 50 percent of Williams graduates marry another Williams student. Scary or not, this says a lot about whether we like each other.

The College Prowler® Grade on

Guys: C-

A high grade for Guys indicates that the male population on campus is attractive, smart, friendly, and engaging, and that the school has a decent ratio of guys to girls.

The College Prowler® Grade on

Girls: C

A high grade for Girls not only implies that the women on campus are attractive, smart, friendly, and engaging, but also that there is a fair ratio of girls to guys.

Athletics

The Lowdown On...
Athletics

Athletic Division:
Division III
Conference: Little Three
NESCAC
ECAC
NCAA

Conference:
New England Small College
Athletic Conference

School Mascot:
Purple Cow

**Males Playing
Varsity Sports:**
380 (39%)

**Females Playing
Varsity Sports:**
284 (29%)

Men's Varsity Sports:

Baseball

Basketball

Cross-Country

Football

Golf

Ice Hockey

Lacrosse

Skiing

Soccer

Swimming & Diving

Tennis

Track & Field (Indoor and Outdoor)

Wrestling

Women's Varsity Sports:

Basketball

Cross-Country

Field Hockey

Ice Hockey

Lacrosse

Rowing

Skiing

Soccer

Softball

Squash

Swimming & Diving

Tennis

Track & Field (Indoor and Outdoor)

Volleyball

Club Sports:

Akido

Badminton

Cycling

Equestrian

Fencing

Figure Skating

Golf

Gymnastics

Rugby (Men's and Women's)

Sailing

Ultimate Frisbee (Men's and Women's)

Volleyball

Water Polo (Men's and Women's)

Intramurals:

Basketball

Flag Football

Soccer

Softball

Volleyball

Getting Tickets

Contact the sports information director at (413) 597-4982.

Most Popular Sports

Football, basketball

Overlooked Teams

Field hockey, tennis

Best Place to Take a Walk

Hopkins Forest

Gyms/Facilities

Bobby Coombs Field

Coombs Field has a permanent outdoor fence, macadam warning track, dugouts, and an extensive drainage system. It is located at the end of Cole Field.

Chandler Athletic Center

The gymnasium in Chandler can accommodate 1,561 for basketball games, in addition to the standing-room-only areas that fill up for NCAA tournament games and the annual clash with Amherst. The volleyball team plays and practices there as well. The gym floor is on the same level as the pool and the trainer's room, which provides the latest in sports medicine, rehabilitation, and injury prevention.

Cole Field

Cole Field is a natural amphitheater that is surrounded by the Berkshire hills and is home to Eph football practice, men's and women's soccer, men's and women's lacrosse, softball, and club rugby teams. Just above the field is Cole Fieldhouse, where teams playing at Cole Field can dress in team locker rooms.

Herbert S. Towne Field House

Towne Field House is a double-domed (technically a "hyperbolic paraboloid") structure that is 252-feet long and 152-feet wide and is used for men's and women's indoor track and men's and women's tennis. It contains a 195-yard Rekortan track, pole vaulting, long-jump and high-jump pits, and a shot put and weight throw area. It also accommodates men's and women's lacrosse, baseball, football, softball, men's and women's tennis and men's and women's soccer in inclement weather or pre-season workouts.

Lansing Chapman Rink

The rink is used for ice hockey and has separate team rooms for the men's and women's teams and a trainer's room. The rink also serves as an indoor training and competition site for men's and women's tennis in the fall and spring.

Lasell Gym

Built in 1886, it serves as a physical education area, practice area for JV basketball, and is the home of Williams wrestling. In addition, it contains an indoor running track, a dance studio, and three golf nets.

Renzie W. Lamb Field

This artificial turf field was dedicated in 2004. Lamb Field serves as the home of Eph field hockey and as a pre-season site for men's and women's lacrosse and home early season games. If Cole Field is unplayable, men's and women's soccer may also utilize the facility.

Simon Squash Center

The center has 12 cement-plaster courts (nine of them glass-backed), coaches' offices, and houses the state-of-the-art Henze Fitness Center.

The Taconic Golf Club

Taconic frequently ranks among the top college-owned courses in the nation and is ranked in the top 100 golf courses in the world. Par is 71 for the 6,614-yard (blue tees), 18-hole course which has hosted several NCAA college tournaments.

Tony Plansky Track

The eight-lane, all-weather track has served as host for NESCAC, ECAC, New England Division III, and New England Division I championships since its installation in 1987. The track can accommodate steeplechase races and has separate high-jump, long-jump, and triple-jump pits. The 400-meter Plansky Track features the action-track surface.

Torrence M. Hunt '44 Tournament Courts

On the north end of campus, the college maintains 18 all-weather and six clay courts for tennis. The outdoor tennis courts have been a popular site for NESCAC Championships and played host to the 1998 NCAA Division III men's championships.

Weston Field

Weston is home to men's and women's outdoor track, football, and since the fall of 2004, field hockey. The seating capacity of the grass football field is 10,000, with ample room for standees and tailgating.

Students Speak Out On...
Athletics

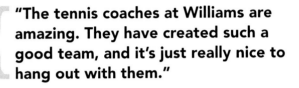

"The tennis coaches at Williams are amazing. They have created such a good team, and it's just really nice to hang out with them."

Q "I am very involved in athletics, on one intramural and one varsity team. I can tell you from experience that the **coaches at Williams are the nicest people on campus**, and they are really good at what they do. Also, the facilities are great. Williams is just the place where you can do the sports that you like, as much as you like, and with people who share your passion."

Q "Athletics are great at Williams. You really learn to be on a team and work with other people to be successful. I think it really makes you a better person, in a way. However, it is a lot of really hard work. I don't blame people who are not on teams for holding a grudge against 'the jocks,' as they call us, because **they just don't have the guts to make the sort of commitment we make every single day** to a group of people and a team activity."

Q "If you are not on an athletic team at Williams, your social life sucks. **Teams have their own parties, which tend to exclude everybody else**. They should put this in the college catalog they send out, because there are many schools out there where this is not the case. Plus, you have the right to know what you are getting into."

Q "I play football, and I like it a lot. **My teammates are great guys, and we win a lot together**. Sometimes we lose, but people learn to support each other in the ups and downs."

Q "It's so cool to be on a team at Williams. You party a lot with your teammates, and you spend most of your time together. Sometimes, we even take the same classes. This is really good as a **bonding experience, and it's a good way to have fun** together with people you know and trust."

Q "It's amazing the money the College spends on building and renovating the sports facilities. They are fantastic. I mean, **I don't even swim that well, but I like being in the pool**. It makes college life healthier:; instead of sleeping in the library, we actually exercise."

Q "I took a class that half of the football team decided to take together. It was painful. They just sat there looking bored and miserable. The professor had to pick on the same three people. I know they win on the football field, but this is no reason for them to take classes together. **They manage to smother whatever spark of intellectual curiosity there is** in this school. I wonder why."

Q "Williams athletes are amazing people. **Many of them play more than one sport and excel academically as well**. They make good friends, because they don't pressure anybody to be like them, and they don't stress about grades either."

Q "If you play a sport, Williams will give you the opportunity to improve your skills, even if it's not the most popular sport—for example, I played field hockey. You have to **work very hard, though, and be a team player**."

Q "**I had a fear of water, and I still learned to swim** thanks to the endless patience and humor of the swim coach, an exceptional professional and a great guy. I used to have trouble even putting my feet in water, and now I actually kind of enjoy it."

Q "The squash and tennis courts at Williams are designed to make you want to play, to be active. **Everything is kept so clean and neat**. It's a pleasure to even just hang out there as a spectator."

Q "Athletics at Williams are on a very high level, rivaling academics, but not making it any less important. People at Williams are dedicated and able; they juggle more than one ball. **There's no reason why you can't be a winner at sports and get good grades**, and learn from both."

Q "**I didn't like the physical education requirement** at Williams. Why should you have to take a certain number of PE classes if it's not really your thing? But the variety of classes offered is so great, and the instructors are so great, that it's all worth taking, from yoga to weight-lifting to squash."

Q "We have to acknowledge that athletic facilities at Williams are not just used by people on the teams, but that everyone enjoys them and has the chance to exercise. **You don't have to be a pro to hang out in the gym and in the pool**, which are just great places to be."

Q "I hadn't participated in many sports before college, and when I started with the crew team at Williams, I wasn't sure how I was going to do. As the year progressed, I found out that my teammates were **ready to welcome both my strengths and my weaknesses**, and that I could do much better than I ever thought."

Q "Sports are really important when you are in college, both for your physical health, but also your sanity, when you are overworked like we tend to be on this campus. **I am glad I was on a team** during my college years, because it helped me build wonderful personal relationships and develop a lot of character."

The College Prowler Take On...
Athletics

Athletics at Williams are for talents and amateurs, for devoted fans and new recruits, for everyone who loves sports, and even for those who might not be that athletic at all. The outstanding professionalism of the coaches and athletic staff makes the wonderful facilities on campus come alive with the spirit and effort of those who learn, teach, compete, play, or just have fun. The variety of sports classes and teams, both varsity and intramural, combined with the quality of their work, has made Williams stand out as a place where athletics thrive.

But do sports take over everything else on campus, pushing aside more intellectual pursuits? Although many would argue this point, one has to acknowledge that sports can only have a positive impact on people, while their individual preference for different activities establishes which activity will prevail. At Williams, many have, in fact, chosen sports over other extracurricular opportunities, and it seems that no one has regretted such a choice.

The College Prowler® Grade on

Athletics: B

A high grade in Athletics indicates that students have school spirit, that sports programs are respected, that games are well-attended, and that intramurals are a prominent part of student life.

Nightlife

The Lowdown On...
Nightlife

Club and Bar Prowler: Popular Nightlife Spots!

Bar Prowler:

Purple Pub
8 Bank Street
Williamstown
(413) 458-3306
www.thepurplepub.com
A great place to hang out and play darts or foosball, grab a bite to eat, or just have a good time.

The Red Herring
46 Spring Street
Williamstown
(413) 458-2808
Journey across the sea to this English pub-style restaurant and bar.

Mezze Bistro & Bar
16 Water Street
Williamstown
(413) 458-0123
www.mezzerestaurant.com
Features live music throughout the year.

Student Favorites:

The Red Herring, Mezze Bistro and Bar

Bars Close At:

1 a.m.

Primary Areas with Nightlife:

Spring Street

Cheapest Place to Get a Drink:

Purple Pub

Favorite Drinking Game:

Beer Pong

What to Do if You're Not 21

Go to parties on campus. You should be fine there, even if you are not 21.

Organization Parties

ACE (All-Campus Entertainment) organizes parties and maintains a calendar of events. Visit *http://ace.williams.edu* to find out the latest information.

Frats

There are no frats at Williams, hence there are no fraternity parties.

Students Speak Out On...
Nightlife

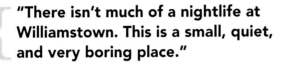

> **"There isn't much of a nightlife at Williamstown. This is a small, quiet, and very boring place."**

Q "If you want nightlife, go to a big city. New York and Boston are not that far. This place was meant to be **a quiet campus for studying and playing sports**. The most fun nights are in dorms and campus parties, though, not in clubs or pubs."

Q "On some nights, **they have cheap beer at Red Herring**. I like that."

Q "Nightlife is what you make it, by going to the liquor shop before it closes and getting together in someone's room when the weather is not too cold, and people are willing to walk over from their corner to yours. It can't really get much more pathetic than that, so think that no matter what you do in terms of social life after you graduate, it will be better than Williams. All of my friends who graduated say so, and they make me optimistic when on Friday night, **I stay in my room buying stuff on the Internet instead of going out**."

Q "**Sometimes we have DJs that come to campus** for parties, and those nights, the music is worth it, but you can't call that nightlife."

Q "It's weird that **people here are not geeky, but they're not the kind of kids who go out too much, either**. That's why we have no nightlife, because both the city and the townspeople just don't care to have one."

Q "Williams does not have much of a nightlife. I have found in my own experience, though, that if you hang out with the right people, you can have a really good time, have parties, and also go out of town to explore places that are just not as quiet as Williamstown. On the other hand, many people in the school and in town are not the kind of people who really want to be up all night in a fancy club. This is why nobody would open one here; it would not be good for their business. I am trying to say that **the town is perfect for the needs and desires of its locals** and most of the college students."

Q **"I am from NYC, so there is no point for me to try to talk about nightlife here.** I don't even know why you are asking this."

Q "Williamstown isn't exactly the center of nightlife in the Berkshires because, honestly, **the Berkshires are not that kind of place**. It's not like if you go to Lee or Lenox or even Pittsfield—at any of those places you would find cool places to go out."

Q "This is New England, my friends; **the Puritans came here and raised cows**. It is not about nightlife."

Q "**Nobody does anything to improve the nightlife**. To me, this means that people don't mind what we have now."

Q "Everybody complains about the lack of nightlife, but I think that campus parties are good enough, and I am not sure that **if there was big club in Williamstown, I would go to it**, when I can get into two or three parties per night without paying."

Q "The question of nightlife really isn't relevant to this place, because it's a small rural town, and you can't expect too much. What the campus has to offer is a different thing, too—not really nightlife, **just your good old college-kids-having-fun-with-kegs-and-Beirut type of thing**. If you don't like it, don't go to college. It's like that everywhere on a college campus."

The College Prowler Take On...
Nightlife

To demand a vibrant nightlife from a town like Williamstown is just not realistic. Most students, even the ones who miss the options of big cities, or are just not satisfied with the Williams way of life, realize that. However, there is a lot to be done in terms of the campus entertainment scene that should not only be a substitute for city nightlife, but is just a separate issue. A huge portion of the entertainment on campus is comprised of stand-up comedy shows and a capella concerts—not exactly the events you can dance and socialize to.

Parties are okay sometimes, and oftentimes, they absolutely suck. Student organizations have put a lot of effort into improving the social scene, but the most tangible results were a couple of concerts with really good bands, once every couple of months. Nevertheless, it is fair to say that there are enough parties one can go to on weekends when the a capella concerts are over.

D

The College Prowler® Grade on
Nightlife: D

A high grade in Nightlife indicates that there are many bars and clubs in the area that are easily accessible and affordable. Other determining factors include the number of options for the under-21 crowd and the prevalence of house parties.

Greek Life

The Lowdown On...
Greek Life

Number of Fraternities:
0

Number of Sororities:
0

Did You Know?

Fraternities were phased out at Williams in the 1960s. However, rumor has it that secret and very exclusive groups form on campus once in a while.

Students Speak Out On...
Greek Life

> **"If we had fraternities, the school would become even more boring and socially handicapped than it already is."**

Q "There are no frats in Williams, which is good, **but we have teams, and they are exclusive enough**."

Q "I am glad there are no frats, but sometimes **I wish we had a way to build more community spirit** and make friends for life. Everyone here is sort of by himself."

Q "I don't know about secret frats. If we have them, **they must be so secret they are insignificant**, because this school is so small that we would have heard."

Q "Williams is a school where peer pressure is brought to a minimum, especially with the lack of frats. I think it's so positive that **you can just be yourself** and not one of many."

Q "Frats were abolished to promote more interaction between different types of students, but this is not really happening, because **we all just find our little niche, anyway**."

Q "I don't know that frats are that bad, but **I really like my life at Williams**, which means that we can do without frats. I think the school should vote on it."

Q "**Fraternities and hazing rituals are horrifying**. They are a thing of the past, and all schools should act like Williams and remove them."

Q "Williams isn't very progressive in many ways, but at least we have no frats. I mean, **we still isolate each other** in little groups, but there is no pressure to be in one, no pressure at all."

Q "Sports teams are bad enough. **They alienate other people and make you stuck with one group**. We don't need fraternities for that in our school."

Q "Fraternities are a thing of the past and should be abolished everywhere. **I don't need a fraternity to make friends in college**, or feel safe because I am part of a group. We are all part of many groups here, whether it's a sports team, the gospel choir, a cultural club, or just sharing the same hobby with others. This is enough to make people feel they are in a community that shares their interests."

Q "I think if we had frats, this place would be even scarier than it already is for people who are not white. I know that the white male jocks would dominate the frat scene and force people into all kinds of unnecessary and embarrassing things. **I think people go to college to learn to be themselves**, not to conform, and to learn to stand up for who they are, even if the majority rejects them outright. Frats on the Williams campus, on the other hand, would show even more how socially isolated this place is, and how it tries to imprison everybody in their own bubble. So maybe if we had them, if this became more evident, and if people became even more miserable, they would do something about it."

Q "I am glad Williams does not have frats. **Frats scare me**."

Q "Not having to deal with fraternity life is part of the reason why I picked Williams over another school. **I think I made the right choice**."

Q "Williams is very progressive for not having frats, but I wonder why some people try to establish them secretly. **I don't want to be a member**."

The College Prowler Take On...
Greek Life

Williams has no Greek life, and most students feel good about this. They find that a fraternity is not the kind of structure they need in order to have a fulfilling college life. Few Williams students would exercise a desire to bond with other students under the authority of a fraternity.

The rumors about a secret fraternity remain a mystery. The idea that sports teams substitute fraternities on campus is also highly debatable, but somewhat confirmed by the fact that teams are often able to live in the same dorm.

The College Prowler® Grade on
Greek Life: N/A

A high grade in Greek Life indicates that sororities and fraternities are not only present, but also active on campus. Other determining factors include the variety of houses available and the respect the Greek community receives from the rest of the campus.

Drug Scene

The Lowdown On...
Drug Scene

Most Prevalent Drugs on Campus:

Alcohol

Marijuana

Liquor-Related Referrals:

24

Liquor-Related Arrests:

0

Drug-Related Referrals:

10

Drug-Related Arrests:

0

Drug Counseling Programs:

Educational workshops offered by Health Center, individual counseling by appointment

Students Speak Out On...
Drug Scene

"People at Williams don't really do drugs. They play too many sports for that. We love alcohol and good cigars, though."

Q "I know **people smoke weed at Williams, but not as much as many other colleges** I have visited. I like that, because nobody is pressured to do anything."

Q "**The social scene at Williams is very divided** between athletes and other people, so you can easily figure out who uses drugs. If you want that, you will be a minority, but you will know from the start who to talk to."

Q "At first **it seems that there is no drug scene at Williams**, but if you look for it, you will find some interesting things, as well as experienced mushroom fans."

Q "**There's like, three people on campus who sell anything**—not much of a choice. The town people are not the kind that will get you good stuff."

Q "Williams kids know how to have fun. If you meet the right people, you can enjoy quality. Quantity isn't sparse, either, **because people can afford pretty much anything**."

Q "I don't know about other drugs, **but the College ostracizes regular smokers**. Fire detectors go off in dorms for no reason, and you can only smoke 25 feet away from any building, which means having a cigarette in the middle of the snow on some lawn and freezing."

Q "Despite the athletic culture of the school, people find ways to enjoy life. **Alcohol is a good thing when it's negative 40 outside**, and an occasional joint helps, too."

Q "There has to be some sort of drug scene at Williams, but I have never seen it, and I'm glad. If you came to college **to learn and stay healthy, Williams is right for you**."

Q "Compared to other campuses I have visited, Williams is almost drug-free. Very **few people smoke tobacco**, too, which is great, even though I sometimes miss the smell of coffee and cigarettes that I grew up with in New York City."

Q "The drug scene at Williams? We have one? **I didn't know that**."

Q "Let's face it: two to three people sell weed on campus, and **everybody who wants some knows who they are**. Not that many people want any, otherwise you would have more dealers for a crowd of over 2,000."

Q "I have to admit, I did my drugs in high school. **I came to Williams to study and have fun** and stay away from them. I have been really successful in doing this, because most of my classmates here really are not into this kind of stuff. I am glad I ended up with them and not some different people."

The College Prowler Take On...
Drug Scene

As most students indicate, there hardly is a drug scene at Williams. Yet, there's always that voice in the corner saying that the drug scene is flourishing if you know where to look.

That's why we are assigning a skeptical A- to this field, hoping that it is actually an A. Meanwhile, we know for a fact that no one would be pressured into doing drugs at Williams, and that those who wish to forget that drugs exist can do so easily on this campus.

The College Prowler® Grade on

Drug Scene: A-

A high grade in the Drug Scene indicates that drugs are not a noticeable part of campus life, drug use is not visible, and no pressure to use them seems to exist.

Campus Strictness

The Lowdown On...
Campus Strictness

What Are You Most Likely to Get Caught Doing on Campus?
- Drinking
- Smoking in dorms

Students Speak Out On...
Campus Strictness

> "You can get drunk on this campus with no worry about someone calling security or the police. Smoking is strictly prohibited, but some fire alarms inside older dorms do not pick up the smoke at all."

Q "This is not a very strict campus. You can't keep candles in your room, **but if you said you needed them for religious reasons, they'd let you do it**. Many people have incense, too, and they smoke in their rooms without having to put something over the smoke detector."

Q "The campus isn't strict. **You can do whatever**, as long as other people around you are fine with it, which works most of the time."

Q "The custodial staff are actually strict, even mean. You can't leave your shoes outside your dorm room, for example, or have anything in the hallways. Storage rules suck, so if you are leaving Williams for the summer, **think twice before you trust the housing office** with anything."

Q "**This is not a strict campus**. Sometimes security would even escort tipsy frosh to their dorm."

Q "The campus is not strict in general, but **there is talk about banning Beirut games and hard alcohol**. I don't know how I feel about that, because I know people will want to keep doing those things."

Q "**JAs (junior advisors) buy alcohol for the frosh**. It's nice of them, but I feel like they should be more responsible."

Q "You can always get past the whole thing of wearing a bracelet to show that you are 21. **So, you can drink at parties, not just in your room or your entry**. Everyone is really chill on the strictness."

Q "I think the campus is as strict as it should be. There really is no reason to become paranoid about what students are going to do, because the regulations are in place, and there are always going to be people who are willing to break them. **I think that at Williams, you do face the consequences of such actions for the most part**, but I also know that college students might not be the most mature people in the world, and so they need some time to grow up and become responsible."

Q "Honestly, people on this campus do not do anything wild enough to test the idea of campus strictness or the people who enforce campus regulations. Beirut games end peacefully, the drug scene is not really prominent, and **many of us are in the library all the time**."

Q "There are strict rules on campus about all kinds of stuff, but I feel like not all rules are taken with the same seriousness. It's kind of random that **you should get a hold on your transcript for lost library books**, but you can buy alcohol for underclassmen and get away with it."

Q "Williams campus strictness? What does that entail? **Kicking me out of the library at 3 a.m. when it closes**?"

Q "This campus is a healthy space, because strict rules are in place; at the same time nobody polices you, though, which is also very important. I think most **people here are responsible and know better than to do drugs**, although Beirut games are not a harmless pleasure either."

The College Prowler Take On...
Campus Strictness

Nobody could really tell us how strict this campus was. Strictness varied with the nature and seriousness of a situation. This statement can be frightening because it implies that the campus strictness is random, and it should not be. Rules should be observed with equal rigor, both when it comes to library policies and underage drinking.

One must weigh the consequences of a late library book versus that of alcohol poisoning, and many feel Williams College security should, too. While Williams has many rules, most students do not find it difficult to follow them.

B+

The College Prowler® Grade on

Campus
Strictness: B+

A high Campus Strictness grade implies an overall lenient atmosphere—police and RAs are fairly tolerant, and the administration's rules are flexible.

Parking

The Lowdown On...
Parking

Williams Parking Services:

Parking is provided for students and faculty with separate lots for each. Visit *http://www.williams.edu/admin/security/rules/vehicle/index.php* for a complete list of vehicle regulations.

Student Parking Lot?

11 student parking lots

Freshmen Allowed to Park?

No

Parking Permit Cost:

$60

Parking Permits:

Parking permits are available to everyone except first-year students. Visitors passes are also available, as well as temporary parking passes that are good for four weeks.

Common Parking Tickets:

Restricted Parking Zone: Warning, then $25

Handicapped Zone: $101

Fire Lane: $101

First-Year Violations: $50

Parking on Grass: Warning, then $50

Did You Know?

Best Places to Find a Parking Spot

Mission and Greylock

Good Luck Getting a Parking Spot Here!

Around Goodrich

Students Speak Out On...
Parking

{ **"If you park far away, you really are wasting time walking from your dorm to the car in the cold, when everything on campus is within walking distance anyway."**

Q "**Parking will depend on your dorm location** and on what building the school decides to destroy or rebuild, making parking spaces into construction fields mined with drills."

Q "Parking is easy in Williamstown. The school allows for visitor parking of friends through **a very quick and easy procedure**."

Q "**Parking is fine**, and people rarely get tickets."

Q "**Consult Williams security before anyone comes to visit you** and parks in the faculty parking, because they might be in trouble."

Q "People with cars should pick the dorms with good parking spaces, which includes many of the dorms. **It also matters who has the spot next to yours**, so look into that before you grab the key."

Q "I have parked in town and on campus, and I've never gotten a ticket. **People are just very chill about parking** issues here."

Q "**Good, safe parking is the advantage of a small town like Willy-town**. By the time you move out after college, you will be way too spoiled to handle Boston traffic, for example."

Q "Well, what sucks is that **freshmen can't bring cars to campus**, so for us, parking is not at all an issue."

Q "I've had to drive and park in Boston a lot, so Williams **seems really peaceful and easy** to me."

Q "Parking used to work fine before Williams started their **huge construction projects**."

Q "**I have no weird parking stories**. It just works fine."

Q "I don't have a car, but some of my friends who do have cars come to visit, and there was **never a problem with visitor's parking**."

Q "Parking might be a problem during family days and other events that just attract many people to town. As far as I remember, though, **even during Homecoming weekend, we didn't have any problems**."

Q "Well, sometimes you might end up parking so far away from your dorm, it makes **you wonder why you didn't just walk up the hill**."

Q "Parking is okay, because Williamstown is just kind of small, but the rules and the paperwork that the buildings and grounds office comes up with can be very annoying. They tend to do everything possible to make your life harder, **so the only way to deal with it is just to be stubborn, and try to make their life harder**. You shouldn't have to fill out a million forms just to park your car. It is a waste of everybody's time."

The College Prowler Take On...
Parking

Parking does not seem to be an issue at Williams, even though it could be improved. When people come to visit, parking becomes very important, so it is nice to know that people are satisfied with their visitor parking passes. The College has been working on ways to provide parking close enough to one's residence so that people wouldn't actually end up walking over to their car for a longer time than they drive it.

As for the construction projects, the consequences are yet to be seen. Nevertheless, parking is not much of an issue, because the campus is so small.

A-

The College Prowler® Grade on

Parking: A-

A high grade in this section indicates that parking is both available and affordable, and that parking enforcement isn't overly severe.

Transportation

The Lowdown On...
Transportation

Ways to Get Around Town:

On Campus

Bike

Walk

Public Transportation

Buses to North Adams and the Berkshire Mall are $1.50 one-way.

Shuttle service to airports provided by Williams College during holidays.

Taxi Cabs

Vet's Taxi
(800) 486-4946

Jenkins Livery
(413) 684-1893 or
(413) 822-6092

Car Rentals

Alamo
(800) 462-5266
www.alamo.com

➜

(Car Rentals, continued)

Enterprise
(800) 261-7331
www.enterprise.com

National
(800) 227-7368
www.nationalcar.com

Thrifty
(800) 847-4389
www.thrifty.com

Airports

Albany International Airport
(1 hour from Williamstown)
(518) 242-2200
www.albanyairport.com

Airlines Serving Albany

Air Canada
(888) 247-2262
www.aircanada.com

Continental
(800) 523-3273
www.continental.com

Delta
(800) 221-1212
www.delta.com

Northwest
(800) 225-2525
http://nwa.com

Southwest
(800) 435-9792
www.southwest.com

United
(800) 241-6522
www.united.com

(Airlines, continued)

US Airways
(800) 428-4322
www.usairways.com

How to Get to the Airport

Bus, car, taxi

A taxi to the airport costs about $90.

Bus Services

Both bus services stop at the Williams Inn on Main Street.

Greyhound

(413) 458-2665
www.greyhound.com

Peter Pan/Bonanza

(800) 751-8800
www.bonanzabus.com

Amtrak

(800) 872-7245
www.amtrak.com

The closest Amtrak station is on Columbus Avenue in Pittsfield, MA, about a half hour from Williamstown.

Travel Agent

The Travel Store, Inc.
620 Main Street
Williamstown
(413) 458-5786

Students Speak Out On...
Transportation

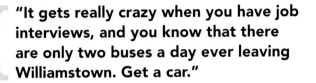

"It gets really crazy when you have job interviews, and you know that there are only two buses a day ever leaving Williamstown. Get a car."

Q "You'll be fine if you drive, but the buses to Billsville are horrible, and no train gets here at all. **Whenever you fly, you have to pay for buses and taxis**, sometimes even taxis all the way from Albany."

Q "The drive to Williamstown is very pretty, but kind of long. Buses take even longer, though, and are very expensive. The good thing is that **the College provides shuttle services over the holidays**."

Q "I can't give you driving directions or anything. I usually fly to Albany from the West Coast, and then I take a cab. It takes forever to get to this place, but at least you can walk to any part of campus, so once you arrive, the most you will need is a bike, at least during the week. If you want to get out of the 'purple bubble,' though, **get a car, or find friends who have access to one**."

Q "Getting to Williams takes forever, even by car, especially if you have to fly to a bigger city first. **The Bonanza and Peter Pan bus services suck big time**. Use them as a last resort to get anywhere."

Q "**I love driving to Williams from Boston**. It's not too long, and it's beautiful in all seasons, even during our super-cold winter."

Q "It gets really hard to drive when **we are snowed in under 20 inches of snow**. But the buses run even then, only taking six to seven hours to NYC instead of the usual five. Wherever you live after college, transportation is likely to be better."

Q "Tickets for the bus coming from Williamstown are more expensive than if you are going. **Always get round-trips** from Boston or New York."

Q "College shuttles are the best transport, because you get to chill with your friends on the bus before you go home for a break or head off to an exotic land. **Those shuttles run on Thanksgiving, Christmas**, spring, and summer holidays. They are pretty fast, and tickets have to be bought well in advance."

Q "**Williamstown is kind of far from everywhere**, but driving to school is not difficult. Even though you can't have a car on campus as a freshman, people will give you rides for just a little bit of gas money, and I know some people who leave campus every weekend, and they take as many other friends as the car can fit."

Q "**It's fairly convenient to fly into Albany airport** and then take a cab or drive, which should also be easier than driving from JFK, or from Logan in Boston."

Q "The only time when transportation might become an issue is when you get bad snowstorms in the winter (winter means you can get them in April or May, too). **Buses usually keep running, though**. Maybe people are used to it. I wouldn't drive by myself with all of this snow."

Q "From the Mass Pike, you can get to Williams fairly quickly. People who have taken the Bonanza bus say it's a terrible experience, but I never have, so **I would just recommend driving**, anyway."

The College Prowler Take On...
Transportation

Get a car as soon as you can, and try to stay away from the bus services. Once you have done that, you should be fine driving to school, leaving town on weekends, and giving the less fortunate first-year students rides to wherever you are going. Driving to Williamstown is pleasant, not confusing, and the roads are good even when you get 30 inches of snow.

As far as flying goes, nobody has an easy time driving out from the major airports in cities like Boston or New York, and the College has done a fair bit to accommodate students who come from those cities by providing a regular, reliable, and relatively cheap shuttle service. While people say that Williams is in the middle of nowhere, the availability of transportation options is not at all discouraging. The College even hires drivers who pick people up from major airports at fairly cheaper prices than most car services would.

The College Prowler® Grade on

Transportation: C-

A high grade for Transportation indicates that campus buses, public buses, cabs, and rental cars are readily-available and affordable. Other determining factors include proximity to an airport and the necessity of transportation.

Weather

The Lowdown On...
Weather

Average Temperature:
Fall: 52°F
Winter: 25°F
Spring: 43°F
Summer: 65°F

Average Precipitation:
Fall: 8.52 in.
Winter: 16.20 in.
Spring: 13.52 in.
Summer: 13.29 in.

Students Speak Out On...
Weather

> **"I came to Williams from Trinidad, and hadn't seen snow before. I can't say I like it, but when you are sitting inside sipping hot chocolate, it's actually beautiful outside."**

Q "It's soooo cold! Even in April, there's snow. **It's too much**."

Q "Most people complain about the weather, but I do lots of skiing, snowboarding, and snowshoeing. **It's actually nice to have good snow for so long**, because you need time on the board to discover the elevations and the semi-filled holes."

Q "The fall in Williamstown is gorgeous with the leaves and everything. **Sometime in October, the cold begins and it ends after—not before—spring break**. I wonder why spring break is called what it's called, because there's no spring around here; the weather goes from cold to very hot and humid."

Q "Buy lots of warm winter clothes—the hardcore kind. You know, those big mittens that make you look like a walking snowman? You're going to need them. **Most people around you will make the same fashion choice**, so you won't feel stupid with your woolen hat, and you should at least be warmed up."

Q "Winter takes so long in Williamstown that you will forget what it's like to walk around campus and not be cold. Spring is very short, and if we have it all, it will be rainy and nasty, with occasional snow and hail. **Summer is the time when you don't want to be on campus anyway**, but if you do stay, you will have to endure the kind of heat that is so humid you can taste it with a spoon. Maybe there are places in the world with worse weather than this, but I just haven't been to them."

Q "Williams is a very small school, and that's good when you have to walk around during the days when the wind chills make the temperature be around negative 40 degrees. On those days, **nothing will save you from being cold**, no matter how many layers you wear. You just have to be patient and wait for these days to pass."

Q "We **never get days off from school for bad weather**, unless the professors who commute from Vermont or some other place just can't drive to campus, which happens once in a while. Students, though, are expected to plough through snow and get to class with frostbite if they have to."

Q "One time I went out with my hair slightly wet, and it turned into frozen sticks. I don't know what else to say. **The cold is overwhelming**."

Q "Williams gets soft and fluffy snow, and it's pretty while it's snowing. **But then it seems to never melt**, and more ice and snow accumulates on top of it on the ground."

Q "Williamstown is absolutely gorgeous in all seasons, especially the fall. **During my sophomore year, we even got an Indian summer** with no snow until early December. It's great for nature lovers. Williamstown is not for people who can't handle the challenge of cold."

Q "It's always winter during the school year in Williamstown. **Learn to like winter if you haven't already**. This is not a normal winter either. It lasts half of the year, at least, and it just makes your bones shiver."

Q "I have gotten used to the cold, and I think Williams is real pretty in the winter. **People just like to whine about the cold**, anyways, because it takes a while for the snow to melt. I think that dressing warm enough solves the problem, and you learn to like the winter landscape a lot."

Q "The fall is gorgeous, and sometimes it lasts long enough for you not to feel that you are freezing all the time. **I also like the beginning of spring in Williamstown**. The summer is too humid, though; it's worse than the winter."

Q "**Williams weather is notoriously cold**, but try some winter sports and some pancakes with maple syrup, and you will be cheered up and filled with enough warmth to get you through all of January and February."

Q "**Williams is beautiful during all seasons**, with all of the trees on campus and the nicely kept lawns. Winter is long, but still pretty; of course, the fall foliage is just gorgeous."

The College Prowler Take On...
Weather

Well, it is cold. It is a matter, though, of how cold is too cold for you? As time goes by, most students learn to cope with the cold, and some actually enjoy the snow. Most wish it was gone by sometime in April when, unfortunately, snowstorms still happen.

The fall is the highlight of Williamstown. Set in the forest and mountain areas of Massachusetts, Williamstown is surrounded by beautiful scenery, even if the weather is a bit chilly. Students find themselves anticipating the coming of spring when the snow finally melts, the weather warms up, and the color returns to Williamstown.

The College Prowler® Grade on

Weather: C-

A high Weather grade designates that temperatures are mild and rarely reach extremes, that the campus tends to be sunny rather than rainy, and that weather is fairly consistent rather than unpredictable.

Report Card Summary

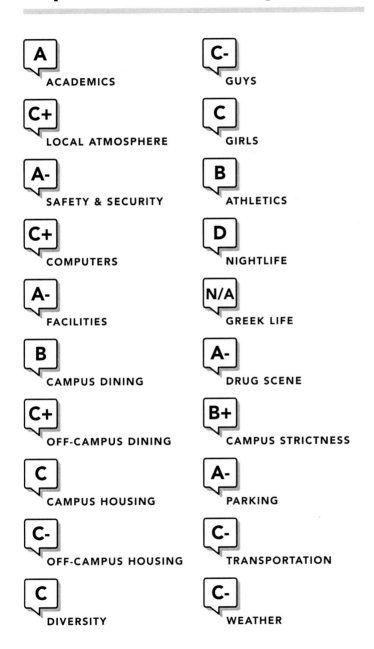

A ACADEMICS	**C-** GUYS
C+ LOCAL ATMOSPHERE	**C** GIRLS
A- SAFETY & SECURITY	**B** ATHLETICS
C+ COMPUTERS	**D** NIGHTLIFE
A- FACILITIES	**N/A** GREEK LIFE
B CAMPUS DINING	**A-** DRUG SCENE
C+ OFF-CAMPUS DINING	**B+** CAMPUS STRICTNESS
C CAMPUS HOUSING	**A-** PARKING
C- OFF-CAMPUS HOUSING	**C-** TRANSPORTATION
C DIVERSITY	**C-** WEATHER

Overall Experience

Students Speak Out On...
Overall Experience

"**Williams is a very liberal institution, and I am not so liberal, so I had a lot of scary thoughts in the beginning about keeping my opinions and expressing them. I now see that my convictions have changed, and this is good.**"

"In four years of school, you'll change a little bit. I see that I have changed other people, too, and that I have been able to stick to what matters the most to me. Professors have been great in this respect; **they let you share, and they don't judge you for standing out** with a different view on popular issues. Clearly, my grades were not impacted by my desire to say what I think, nor did I feel alienated, although I was always a minority."

Q "After four years at Williams, I don't really feel ready for the real world, just because Williams is not the real world. Williams is a place that shelters you from the world in many ways, and it tries to educate you in a very thorough, but not necessarily practical, way. I had a very good time attending classes, hanging out with friends, and just being myself here, because there was so little pressure to deal with the external reality of things. **I know that Williams is also a place that tries to help you in many ways** to find a job, but the range of jobs you can seek is limited. When you start, you get to see for yourself that you are not prepared, which actually might be true for any other college graduate. But I know that Williams has been excellent for me academically, and I always felt supported and just appreciated by people here. I was able to work on my own strengths, too, at a fairly intense pace, but a pace that I think my own goals set for me."

Q "I respect Williams tremendously for providing me with an environment where I could learn and not worry about anything else. Also, it was very important to me to continue playing sports, and Williams gave me this opportunity. I think that Williams is a school where you must work very hard to achieve your goals and to be satisfied with your results, but I think people choose to pressure themselves to work hard, because that is who they are. For example, **I know nobody forced me into waking up at 6 a.m. for practice** and then rushing to a 9 a.m. class. I felt that the people around me respected my ambitions and my schedule, and no one tried to change me. I found many people I can relate to."

Q "Williams is great—if you are white and rich. I realize this is true of many other places. I know, though, that **the College has tried to make those of us who are not white and rich feel at home**. I wish other students, too, could have this in mind, not just the institution. Socially, I was always in a group of friends from the same race as myself. Maybe this was a good thing. Who knows? But then I thought 'Gee, I am supposed to be expanding my horizons.' So I am kind of confused about how college should work to make you a more open person by exposing you to different stuff. They expose you, but it doesn't mean you interact with the others. You kind of know they are there, and they know you are there and choose to ignore you way too often."

Q "Williams was the perfect place for me to keep up on my interests and passions from high school. I think I picked up a few new ones, too, and really learned a lot in my major because of the great faculty we have here. I like this place so much, and I am not ready to leave at all, because I always feel like I am learning. I felt that someone was there for me all the time for support when I needed it. **What matters the most are my professors, my coaches, and my friends** who accept me as I am and stand by me without making me less independent. I know my parents were impressed with how much I changed when I came home the summer after freshman year. You just don't notice some stuff like that, because you are wrapped up in your work, but my family added lots of perspective that way, and they felt just like I did: that I picked the right school."

Q "I had a lot of fun at Williams. I didn't study too hard, I made many friends, enjoyed the beautiful campus, and played a lot of Frisbee. Just kidding. This is a great place to be, even though it gets too calm and boring at times, because the town is so small. However, it's great if you have a small group of good friends and **you develop very strong bonds with them that will last for as long as anything in your life**. About classes: this is the place to be if you want to get lots of personal attention. The living situation might not always be the best; the Williams housing office will do anything to make your life hard, and when they do, you have to stand up for yourself instead of expecting any integrity from them."

Q "Williams is better than Amherst. We all know that. It is better than many other schools, too. One of my friends thinks Williams gets all the Harvard rejects, but he is a Harvard reject himself, and I applied here for early decision. I didn't choose the school because of the name but instead for the beautiful campus, and **it just seemed like the right people were here for me**. Williams doesn't have the Harvard reputation, and most people won't know where you went to school. You're going to find out that this is the right place when you see how well they treat you and how much freedom they give for choosing classes. The core curriculum here is very flexible, and you really can design your own plan of what to do with four years of being among the brightest kids in the country. The professors are just awesome, too."

Q "Everything here is great, but your social life sucks; it's just so limited. I never had a relationship at Williams, and most of my friends didn't either. It can get very lonely and depressing. You have to do work all the time, and if you don't, there is nothing else to do. **People care about their grades and their sports too much** to notice others and be friends with them. If you are gay, your love life is extremely limited, and it doesn't get much better for the straight people, either. People look for sex, but not for any meaningful interaction. Most are too immature to appreciate another person."

Q "Some of the people here are very selfish and arrogant, especially the jocks who can be very aggressive at parties and they think they just own this campus when they don't. **The rest of us don't enjoy anything of what they get**. They live in the best dorms and get drunk all the time, and they make too much noise for anyone to study, sleep, or just chill in their own room. Most of the school's money goes for the athletic teams when there are so many cool things to do, like research. People are very boring. Four years in a top school doesn't make them more open-minded, just more hypocritical and snobbish."

Q "It all seems great before you try to find a job. You see that **if you don't want to go straight to Wall Street, you are stuck**; hardly anyone recruits on this campus except investment banks and some consulting companies—very few, actually. Needless to say, you have to be very white and athletic for any of those jobs. Should the rest of us go wait tables at corporate lounges? No. You can't do that either, because those places require waitress experience, not a college degree. Go to graduate school? What if you want to take a break from homework and tests and actually make some money so you can pay for your next degree?"

The College Prowler Take On...
Overall Experience

It is very hard to get an A at Williams, so most are happy with a B+ or an A-. The same logic applies to what the school has to offer students. Williams is amazing for its incredible academic and athletic programs. However, the lack of diversity among the student body is detrimental for students' social lives and personal growth. It is for that reason this school cannot receive an A or A-. The students who completed the surveys did acknowledge that some of the weaknesses of the school, such as location and the nature of nightlife in Williamstown, are not fixable. They also agreed that Williams is working very hard on addressing other problematic issues. While the school changes with every class and every year, some positive and negative aspects of what it has to offer to the prospective student stand out as worth mentioning. These are not only conditions that can't be changed, like the weather, but also general features of Williams that many students criticize or praise.

No matter what the admissions office tries to tell you, the Williams campus is not particularly diverse. Many students of color feel very alienated here, and so do white students who don't necessary fit the typical preppy profile. Many blame the lack of diversity to the school's focus on athletics, but I think that this just isn't fair to the Williams sports teams, who do so much to promote the school's spirit. Choosing one group of people over another is a choice on behalf of the admissions counsel. It is thought that maybe Williams lacks in diversity because it has already been associated as a typically "white and preppy" school. Besides admitting a fairly uniform and uninteresting student body, Williams has also placed them in a small and uninteresting town, where their social life is limited to keg parties with the same group of people every weekend and occasional dancing to the same three songs. Although many complain about this, others like those three songs and the beer, and they don't require more options.

The Inside Scoop

The Lowdown On...
The Inside Scoop

Things I Wish I Knew Before Coming to Williams College

- Williamstown is so far from any place where you could go out at night.
- No matter what they tell you about the cold weather at Williams, you would always wish you knew more about how cold it actually can get.
- There's a flimsy veil of political correctness behind which the school attempts to disguise a lot of very disturbing sentiments among the student body.
- Many students wish they knew more about the mind-boggling amount of work they are expected to do every week in almost all majors.
- The housing office will play any joke on them at any time, like kick them out of their dorm during the week of finals because construction is going on.

Tips to Succeed at Williams College

- Talk to your professors. Sometimes they face the same issues as you do.
- Talk to alumni. They, for sure, have faced the same issues as you, especially with finding jobs and internships.
- Don't start a senior thesis unless you are sure you are in love with your topic and can handle it for as long as a lifetime.
- Don't start a thesis in the political science department, even if you are in love with your topic. Just make sure the faculty are in love with it.
- Pick your classes carefully. Read about the professors who teach them, and ask students who took the classes before.
- If you are an international student, take economics to prepare for the job market that Williams exposes you to.
- Do not assume that Williams is boring if you are not a jock.
- Avoid conflict with the librarians in Sawyer, especially if you have something overdue. You might lose some hair or teeth in a battle with the librarians.
- Take advantage of the excellent sports facilities, even if you are not into sports.
- Go abroad junior year. Or some summer.
- Don't take Williams for granted. It is a place where many good people work to make you a better person.
- Don't blame it on Williams if you don't think you are becoming a better person.
- Go skiing to battle the cold.

Williams Urban Legends

The Williams Snack Bar staff are among the campus's urban legends. When students see them wearing normal clothes, they usually react like they just saw Star Trek officers wearing jeans. The amount of work that these people do with a smile on their face rivals even the hours the geekiest math major spends in the library.

Is it a legend that somewhere in the deep basement of Bronfman, the psych students performed experiments on their own brains? Does that mean they had brains to begin with? Bronfman is certainly a spooky building.

(Urban Legends, continued)

The health center is also known for giving out free condoms. But some will tell you, and others will confirm, that those condoms break. For those who spent most of their time hiding from the noisy air-conditioner in Sawyer library, this is just a legend.

Have people had sex in the two-level monkey carrels in Sawyer Library? One witness told me he has seen lesbian sex. What remains a mystery is how the library workers, who are all eyes and ears, did not see it. Another Sawyer legend has it that students hid in the library and slept there after security locked up all the doors.

School Spirit

Mucho Macho Moocow Marching Band is the cheering section at football games and a big provider of school spirit.

Traditions

Class Banners
Each class designs a banner that will represent them while at school and at reunions in the future.

Ivy Planting
At graduation, a member of the graduating class plants ivy next to a wall or a building.

The Mountains
The College alma mater, composed by Williams graduate Washington Gladden, puts the setting of Williams into words.

Watch Dropping
Also at graduation, a watch is dropped from the top of the college chapel. If the watch breaks, the graduating class will be lucky.

Finding a Job or Internship

The Lowdown On...
Finding a Job or Internship

The Office of Career Counseling (OCC) offers programs for students and alumni. From resumé writing to applying for jobs, the OCC is ready to help students in after-college pursuits. Many students feel that the OCC does not provide for all majors or career paths. However, they offer online resumé posting and links to many job searches.

Office of Career Counseling
Williams College
Stetson Hall LL
Williamstown, MA 01267
(413) 597.2311
occ@williams.edu
www.williams.edu/resources/occ

OCC Services

Williams OCC offers walk-in career counseling Monday–Friday between 11 a.m. and 3 p.m. Counselors are available for quick answers to quick questions, and questions are answered on a first-come, first-serve basis. Students are encouraged to make appointments, even if they are still unsure of their future plans, to discuss their options and have mock interviews.

The OCC also publishes many guides, including *The New Lephlet*, to help students prepare for interviews and tests. There is also a resource library and workshops to help students in their search.

Alumni

The Lowdown On...
Alumni

Web Site:
www.williams.edu/alumni

Office:
75 Park Street
Williamstown
(413) 597-3545

Major Alumni Events:
For a full list of alumni events,
please see the calendar at
*www.williams.edu/alum
ni/news.*

Services Available:
Alumni directory
Alumni travel-study
Career network
E-mail groups
Permanent e-mail
Ride board

Did You Know?

Famous Williams Alumni

Steve Case – Founder and former CEO of America Online

John Frankenheimer – Director of *The Manchurian Candidate* and other notable films

James Garfield – Former President of the United States

Reza Pahlavi II – Former Crown Prince of Iran, matriculated at Williams, but left after his freshman year due to the Islamic Revolution led by Ayatollah Khomeini

Student Organizations

For information on Williams College student organizations, visit *http://wso.williams.edu/organizations*.

Accidentals
African Students Organization (WASO)
Aikikan
All Campus Entertainment (ACE)
Anchors Away
Anime Club
Anti-Gravity Society
Asian Dance Troupe
Asian Theater Project (ATP)
Asian American Students in Action (AASiA)
Astronomy Club
Badminton Club
Berkshire Symphony
Biology Majors Advisory Committee (BMAC)
Black Student Union (WBSU)
Bone Marrow Registry Organization
Brass Ensemble
Bridge Club
Canboulay

Cap and Bells

Capoeira

Ceramics Club

Chamber Choir

Chess Club

Chinese American Student Organization (CASO)

Chocolate Appreciation Society

Christian Fellowship (WCF)

Cinephiles

Clarinet Choir

College Bowl

College Council (Student Government)

Combination Pizza

Community Building Program (WCBP)

Competitive Eating Organization

Concert Choir

Cricket Club

Culture Counter

Curling Club

Cycling Team

Dance Company: A Modern Dance Ensemble

Dancesport Club

Dancing Folk

Debate Team, Williams College Parliamentary

Democrats@Williams

Dissonance

Double Sixes at Williams

Elizabethans

Ephlats

Ephoria

Equestrian Team

Essence

Feast

Feminist Alliance (WFA)

Fencing Club

Figure Skating Club

First-Year (Frosh) Student Council

Flute Choir

Forest Garden

Francophone and Francophile Club (French)

Free University

Gaming Alliance

Gargoyle Society

Good Question

Gospel Choir

Grassroots Music

Greensense

Gulielmensian (Gul), The

Gymnastics Club

Habitat for Humanity

Handbell Choir

Harrison Morgan Brown Pre-Medical Society (HMBPS)

Hawai'i 'Ohana

House Coordinators (and other Campus Life Team members)

Independent Horns

International Club (WIC)

International Justice Journal (IJJ)

Investment Club

Italian American Club

Jazz Ensemble

Jewish Association (WCJA)

Koreans of Williams (KOW)

Kusika: African Dance, Music, and Storytelling Ensemble

Lehman Community Service Council

Literary Review

Literary Society (Unbound Literary Magazine)

Mad Cow Humor Society

Martial Arts Club

Meditation Society

Minority Coalition (MinCo)

Moocho Macho Moocow Military Marching Band

Museum Associates Program

Musical Pedagogy Association

Muslim Student Union (MSU)

Nothin' But Cuties (NBC)

Octet

Outing Club (WOC)

Peer Health

Percussion Ensemble

Photography Club

Poppers

Prizm

Purple Bike Coalition

Purple Key Society

Queer Student Union (QSU)

Rape and Sexual Assault Network

Republican Club

Role Players (WARP)

Rotaract Club

Rude Cider

Run for a Cure

Sailing Team

Samulnori Club

Sankofa: The Williams College Step Team

Scattershot

Snowboarding Club

Sol Ka Fe

South Asian Students Association (SASA)

Spanish Club

Springstreeters

String/Piano Chamber Music

Student Centers Management Team (Goodrich and the Log)

Student Global AIDS Campaign

Student Symphony

Students for Organ Donor Awareness (SODA)

Students for Sensible Drug Policy

Students for Social Justice

Students of Caribbean Ancestry (SoCA)

Students of Mixed Heritage (SoMH)

Sushi Club

Swing Club

Symphonic Winds

Timeline Productions

Ultimate Frisbee Organization (WUFO) (Men's)

Ultimate Frisbee Organization (WUFO) (Women's)

Vietnamese Students Association (VISA)

Vista

Voice for Choice

WCFM Williamstown 91.9 FM

Williams Catholic

Williams Christian Fellowship

Williams College Model United Nations

Williams Entrepreneurship Society

Williams for Life

Williams Forensics Society

Williams Magic: The Gathering Club

Williams Music Swap

Williams Rocket Club

Williams Students Online (WSO)

Williams Trivia

Woodwind Chamber Music

Writing Workshop

Youth Vote

Zambezi Marimba Band

The Best & Worst

The Ten BEST Things About Williams

1 The professors' willingness to give personal attention

2 The facilities

3 Being on a sports team

4 A very flexible core curriculum

5 Study abroad opportunities

6 Tutorials

7 The JA system

8 Administration is extremely helpful

9 Big single rooms with huge windows and private baths

10 Beautiful campus

The Ten WORST Things About Williams

1 Lack of diversity

2 Limited social life due to geographic isolation

3 Transportation to Williams

4 Heating in dorms

5 The computer network

6 Very cold weather

7 Limited selection of classes in some departments

8 Overemphasizing career opportunities and rejecting others

9 The housing office and the housing lottery

10 The swim requirement

Visiting

The Lowdown On...
Visiting

Hotel Information:

Best Value Inn
5939 Route 7 North
Pownal
(802) 823-7341
Distance From Campus:
4.5 miles
Price Range: $61–$159

Chimney Mirror Motel
295 Main Street, Rt. 2
Williamstown
(413) 458-5202
Distance from Campus: 1 mile
Price Range: $55–$70

Four Acres Motel

213 Main Street
Williamstown

(413) 458-8258

Distance from Campus: 1 mile

Price: $69–$145

The House on Main Street

1120 Main Street
Williamstown

(413) 458-3031

www.houseonmainstreet.com

Distance from Campus: 1 mile

Price Range: $85–$150

Maple Terrace Motel

555 Main Street
Williamstown

(413) 458-9677

Distance from Campus: 1 mile

Price Range: $55–$145

Northside Motel

45 North Street
Williamstown

(413) 458-8107

Distance from Campus: 1 mile

Price Range: $89

The Orchards

222 Adams Road
Williamstown

800) 225-1517

www.orchardshotel.com

Distance from Campus: 1 mile

Price Range: $175–$450

The Porches Inn

231 River Street
North Adams

Distance from Campus: 5 miles

Price Range: $299

The Williams Inn

1090 Main Street
Williamstown

(413) 458-9371

Distance from Campus: 1 mile

Price Range: $135–$260

Take a Campus Virtual Tour

www.williams.edu/admission/vtour/index.html

To Schedule a Group Information Session or Interview

No appointment is necessary for an information session. Sessions last about three hours and are lead by admissions staff.

Interviews focusing on student questions are available from 9 a.m. to 3:30 p.m. from May to September. Alumni interviews can also be scheduled until November. To schedule an interview, call (413) 597-2214 or visit *www.williams.edu/admission/visit_interviews.php* for more information.

Campus Tours

No advanced notice is needed for a campus tour. Tours generally last one hour and are lead by students.

For more information on group sessions or campus tours, including holiday tour schedules, please visit *www.williams.edu/admission/visit_tours.php*.

Overnight Visits

High school seniors are eligible to stay overnight at Williams. Overnight visits are arranged through the Purple Key Society and the admissions office and are available Sunday through Thursday nights starting in October. Visits must be scheduled at least 10 days in advance. Please call the admissions office for more information, or visit *www.williams.edu/admission/visit_overnight.php* to schedule online.

Directions to Campus

Driving from the North
- Route 7 South to Route 2
- Turn left on Route 2 East

Driving from the South
- I-87 North to I-84 East
- I-84 East to the Taconic Parkway North
- Taconic Parkway North to Route 295 East
- Route 295 East to Route 22 North
- Route 22 North to Route 43 East
- Route 43 East to Route 7 North
- Route 7 North to Route 2 East

Driving from the East
- Route 2 West all the way to Williamstown

or
- Mass Pike (I-90) West to Lee (exit 2)
- Route 20 West to Route 7 North
- Route 7 North to Route 2 East

Driving from the West
- Route 7 East to Route 278
- Turn right on Route 278 to Route 2
- Turn left on Route 2 East

From Bradley International Airport (Hartford, CT)
- Follow signs to I-91 North
- Exit on Mass Pike (I-90) West to Lee (exit 2)
- Route 20 West to Route 7 North
- Route 7 North to Route 2 East

From the Albany International Airport
- At airport exit turn left
- Follow signs to I-87 North (Northway to Montreal)
- Exit Route 7 East to Route 278
- Turn right on Route 278 to Route 2
- Turn left on Route 2 East

Words to Know

Academic Probation – A suspension imposed on a student if he or she fails to keep up with the school's minimum academic requirements. Those unable to improve their grades after receiving this warning can face dismissal.

Beer Pong/Beirut – A drinking game involving cups of beer arranged in a pyramid shape on each side of a table. The goal is to get a ping pong ball into one of the opponent's cups by throwing the ball or hitting it with a paddle. If the ball lands in a cup, the opponent is required to drink the beer.

Bid – An invitation from a fraternity or sorority to 'pledge' (join) that specific house.

Blue-Light Phone – Brightly-colored phone posts with a blue light bulb on top. These phones exist for security purposes and are located at various outside locations around most campuses. In an emergency, a student can pick up one of these phones (free of charge) to connect with campus police or a security escort.

Campus Police – Police who are specifically assigned to a given institution. Campus police are typically not regular city officers; they are employed by the university in a full-time capacity.

Club Sports – A level of sports that falls somewhere between varsity and intramural. If a student is unable to commit to a varsity team but has a lot of passion for athletics, a club sport could be a better, less intense option. Even less demanding, intramural (IM) sports often involve no traveling and considerably less time.

Cocaine – An illegal drug. Also known as "coke" or "blow," cocaine often resembles a white crystalline or powdery substance. It is highly addictive and dangerous.

Common Application – An application with which students can apply to multiple schools.

Course Registration – The period of official class selection for the upcoming quarter or semester. Prior to registration, it is best to prepare several back-up courses in case a particular class becomes full. If a course is full, students can place themselves on the waitlist, although this still does not guarantee entry.

Division Athletics – Athletic classifications range from Division I to Division III. Division IA is the most competitive, while Division III is considered to be the least competitive.

Dorm – A dorm (or dormitory) is an on-campus housing facility. Dorms can provide a range of options from suite-style rooms to more communal options that include shared bathrooms. Most first-year students live in dorms. Some upperclassmen who wish to stay on campus also choose this option.

Early Action – An application option with which a student can apply to a school and receive an early acceptance response without a binding commitment. This system is becoming less and less available.

Early Decision – An application option that students should use only if they are certain they plan to attend the school in question. If a student applies using the early decision option and is admitted, he or she is required and bound to attend that university. Admission rates are usually higher among students who apply through early decision, as the student is clearly indicating that the school is his or her first choice.

Ecstasy – An illegal drug. Also known as "E" or "X," ecstasy looks like a pill and most resembles an aspirin. Considered a party drug, ecstasy is very dangerous and can be deadly.

Ethernet – An extremely fast Internet connection available in most university-owned residence halls. To use an Ethernet connection properly, a student will need a network card and cable for his or her computer.

Fake ID – A counterfeit identification card that contains false information. Most commonly, students get fake IDs with altered birthdates so that they appear to be older than 21 (and therefore of legal drinking age). Even though it is illegal, many college students have fake IDs in hopes of purchasing alcohol or getting into bars.

Frosh – Slang for "freshman" or "freshmen."

Hazing – Initiation rituals administered by some fraternities or sororities as part of the pledging process. Many universities have outlawed hazing due to its degrading, and sometimes dangerous, nature.

Intramurals (IMs) – A popular, and usually free, sport league in which students create teams and compete against one another. These sports vary in competitiveness and can include a range of activities—everything from billiards to water polo. IM sports are a great way to meet people with similar interests.

Keg – Officially called a half-barrel, a keg contains roughly 200 12-ounce servings of beer.

LSD – An illegal drug, also known as acid, this hallucinogenic drug most commonly resembles a tab of paper.

Marijuana – An illegal drug, also known as weed or pot; along with alcohol, marijuana is one of the most commonly-found drugs on campuses across the country.

Major –The focal point of a student's college studies; a specific topic that is studied for a degree. Examples of majors include physics, English, history, computer science, economics, business, and music. Many students decide on a specific major before arriving on campus, while others are simply "undecided" until declaring a major. Those who are extremely interested in two areas can also choose to double major.

Meal Block – The equivalent of one meal. Students on a meal plan usually receive a fixed number of meals per week. Each meal, or "block," can be redeemed at the school's dining facilities in place of cash. Often, a student's weekly allotment of meal blocks will be forfeited if not used.

Minor – An additional focal point in a student's education. Often serving as a complement or addition to a student's main area of focus, a minor has fewer requirements and prerequisites to fulfill than a major. Minors are not required for graduation from most schools; however some students who want to explore many different interests choose to pursue both a major and a minor.

Mushrooms – An illegal drug. Also known as "'shrooms," this drug resembles regular mushrooms but is extremely hallucinogenic.

Off-Campus Housing – Housing from a particular landlord or rental group that is not affiliated with the university. Depending on the college, off-campus housing can range from extremely popular to non-existent. Students who choose to live off campus are typically given more freedom, but they also have to deal with possible subletting scenarios, furniture, bills, and other issues. In addition to these factors, rental prices and distance often affect a student's decision to move off campus.

Office Hours – Time that teachers set aside for students who have questions about coursework. Office hours are a good forum for students to go over any problems and to show interest in the subject material.

Pledging – The early phase of joining a fraternity or sorority, pledging takes place after a student has gone through rush and received a bid. Pledging usually lasts between one and two semesters. Once the pledging period is complete and a particular student has done everything that is required to become a member, that student is considered a brother or sister. If a fraternity or a sorority would decide to "haze" a group of students, this initiation would take place during the pledging period.

Private Institution – A school that does not use tax revenue to subsidize education costs. Private schools typically cost more than public schools and are usually smaller.

Prof – Slang for "professor."

Public Institution – A school that uses tax revenue to subsidize education costs. Public schools are often a good value for in-state residents and tend to be larger than most private colleges.

Quarter System (or Trimester System) – A type of academic calendar system. In this setup, students take classes for three academic periods. The first quarter usually starts in late September or early October and concludes right before Christmas. The second quarter usually starts around early to mid–January and finishes up around March or April. The last academic quarter, or "third quarter," usually starts in late March or early April and finishes up in late May or Mid-June. The fourth quarter is summer. The major difference between the quarter system and semester system is that students take more, less comprehensive courses under the quarter calendar.

RA (Resident Assistant) – A student leader who is assigned to a particular floor in a dormitory in order to help to the other students who live there. An RA's duties include ensuring student safety and providing assistance wherever possible.

Recitation – An extension of a specific course; a review session. Some classes, particularly large lectures, are supplemented with mandatory recitation sessions that provide a relatively personal class setting.

Rolling Admissions – A form of admissions. Most commonly found at public institutions, schools with this type of policy continue to accept students throughout the year until their class sizes are met. For example, some schools begin accepting students as early as December and will continue to do so until April or May.

Room and Board – This figure is typically the combined cost of a university-owned room and a meal plan.

Room Draw/Housing Lottery – A common way to pick on-campus room assignments for the following year. If a student decides to remain in university-owned housing, he or she is assigned a unique number that, along with seniority, is used to determine his or her housing for the next year.

Rush – The period in which students can meet the brothers and sisters of a particular chapter and find out if a given fraternity or sorority is right for them. Rushing a fraternity or a sorority is not a requirement at any school. The goal of rush is to give students who are serious about pledging a feel for what to expect.

Semester System – The most common type of academic calendar system at college campuses. This setup typically includes two semesters in a given school year. The fall semester starts around the end of August or early September and concludes before winter vacation. The spring semester usually starts in mid-January and ends in late April or May.

Student Center/Rec Center/Student Union – A common area on campus that often contains study areas, recreation facilities, and eateries. This building is often a good place to meet up with fellow students; depending on the school, the student center can have a huge role or a non-existent role in campus life.

Student ID – A university-issued photo ID that serves as a student's key to school-related functions. Some schools require students to show these cards in order to get into dorms, libraries, cafeterias, and other facilities. In addition to storing meal plan information, in some cases, a student ID can actually work as a debit card and allow students to purchase things from bookstores or local shops.

Suite – A type of dorm room. Unlike dorms that feature communal bathrooms shared by the entire floor, suites offer bathrooms shared only among the suite. Suite-style dorm rooms can house anywhere from two to ten students.

TA (Teacher's Assistant) – An undergraduate or grad student who helps in some manner with a specific course. In some cases, a TA will teach a class, assist a professor, grade assignments, or conduct office hours.

Undergraduate – A student in the process of studying for his or her bachelor's degree.

ABOUT THE AUTHOR

Alexandra Grashkina, known as Alex or Sasha, was born 06/06/1981 in Sofia, Bulgaria. She attended an American high school called ACS (American College of Sofia) and traveled to New York City as an exchange student when she was 16. Ever since, she decided that traveling was a good thing and packed her suitcase every four months or so.

Later on, she studied social sciences and languages in Williams College, Williamstown, in Fortaleza, Brazil and in Geneva, Switzerland. Alex speaks English, Bulgarian, Russian, French, and Portuguese with very little difficulty and has intermediate knowledge of Spanish and Italian. She is now learning the Armenian alphabet.

To Williams College, Alex owes a lot, but her biggest achievement was overcoming her fear of water and somewhat learning to swim.

Currently, she works as a paralegal in civil litigation and is trying to stay out of trouble when not at work.

Alexandra Grashkina
alexandragrashkina@collegeprowler.com

California Colleges

California dreamin'?
This book is a must have for you!

CALIFORNIA COLLEGES
7¼" X 10", 762 Pages Paperback
$29.95 Retail
1-59658-501-3

Stanford, UC Berkeley, Caltech—California is home to some of America's greatest institutes of higher learning. *California Colleges* gives the lowdown on 24 of the best, side by side, in one prodigious volume.

New England Colleges

Looking for peace in the Northeast?
Pick up this regional guide to New England!

NEW ENGLAND COLLEGES
7¼" X 10", 1015 Pages Paperback
$29.95 Retail
1-59658-504-8

New England is the birthplace of many prestigious universities, and with so many to choose from, picking the right school can be a tough decision. With inside information on over 34 competive Northeastern schools, *New England Colleges* provides the same high-quality information prospective students expect from College Prowler in one all-inclusive, easy-to-use reference.

Schools of the South

Headin' down south? This book will help you find your way to the perfect school!

SCHOOLS OF THE SOUTH
7¼" X 10", 773 Pages Paperback
$29.95 Retail
1-59658-503-X

Southern pride is always strong. Whether it's across town or across state, many Southern students are devoted to their home sweet home. *Schools of the South* offers an honest student perspective on 36 universities available south of the Mason-Dixon.

Untangling
the Ivy League

The ultimate book for everything Ivy!

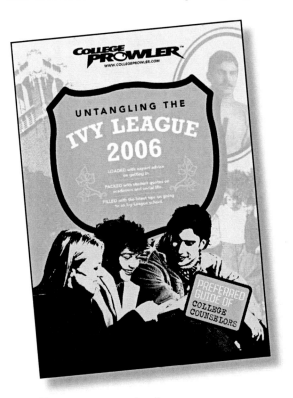

UNTANGLING THE IVY LEAGUE
7¼" X 10", 567 Pages Paperback
$24.95 Retail
1-59658-500-5

Ivy League students, alumni, admissions officers, and other top insiders get together to tell it like it is. *Untangling the Ivy League* covers every aspect—from admissions and athletics to secret societies and urban legends—of the nation's eight oldest, wealthiest, and most competitive colleges and universities.

Need Help Paying For School?

Apply for our scholarship!

College Prowler awards thousands of dollars a year to students who compose the best essays. E-mail scholarship@collegeprowler.com for more information, or call 1-800-290-2682.

Apply now at ***www.collegeprowler.com***

Tell Us What Life Is Really Like at Your School!

Have you ever wanted to let people know what your college is really like? Now's your chance to help millions of high school students choose the right college.

Let your voice be heard.

Check out **www.collegeprowler.com** for more info!

Need More Help?

Do you have more questions about this school?
Can't find a certain statistic? College Prowler is
here to help. We are the best source of college
information out there. We have a network
of thousands of students who can get the latest
information on any school to you ASAP.
E-mail us at info@collegeprowler.com with your
college-related questions.

E-Mail Us Your College-Related Questions!

Check out ***www.collegeprowler.com*** for more details.
1-800-290-2682

Write For Us!
Get published! Voice your opinion.

Writing a College Prowler guidebook is both fun and
rewarding; our open-ended format allows your own
creativity free reign. Our writers have been featured
in national newspapers and have seen their names in
bookstores across the country. Now is your chance
to break into the publishing industry with one of the
country's fastest-growing publishers!

Apply now at *www.collegeprowler.com*

Contact editor@collegeprowler.com or
call 1-800-290-2682 for more details.

Pros and Cons

Still can't figure out if this is the right school for you?
You've already read through this in-depth guide; why not
list the pros and cons? It will really help with narrowing down
your decision and determining whether or not
this school is right for you.

Pros	Cons
....	....
....	....
....	....
....	....
....	....
....	....
....	....
....	....
....	....
....	....
....	....
....	....
....	....

Pros and Cons

Still can't figure out if this is the right school for you?
You've already read through this in-depth guide; why not
list the pros and cons? It will really help with narrowing down
your decision and determining whether or not
this school is right for you.

Pros	Cons
....	....
....	....
....	....
....	....
....	....
....	....
....	....
....	....
....	....
....	....
....	....
....	....
....	....

Notes

Notes

Notes

Notes

....

....

....

....

....

....

....

....

....

....

....

....

....

Notes

Notes

Notes

....

....

....

....

....

....

....

....

....

....

....

....

....

Notes

....

....

....

....

....

....

....

....

....

....

....

....

....

....

Notes

Notes

Notes

Notes

Notes

....

....

....

....

....

....

....

....

....

....

....

....

....

....

Notes

Notes

....

....

....

....

....

....

....

....

....

....

....

....

....

Notes

....

....

....

....

....

....

....

....

....

....

....

....

....

Notes

Albion College
Alfred University
Allegheny College
American University
Amherst College
Arizona State University
Auburn University
Babson College
Ball State University
Bard College
Barnard College
Bates College
Baylor University
Beloit College
Bentley College
Binghamton University
Birmingham Southern College
Boston College
Boston University
Bowdoin College
Brandeis University
Brigham Young University
Brown University
Bryn Mawr College
Bucknell University
Cal Poly
Cal Poly Pomona
Cal State Northridge
Cal State Sacramento
Caltech
Carleton College
Carnegie Mellon University
Case Western Reserve
Centenary College of Louisiana
Centre College
Claremont McKenna College
Clark Atlanta University
Clark University
Clemson University
Colby College
Colgate University
College of Charleston
College of the Holy Cross
College of William & Mary
College of Wooster
Colorado College
Columbia University
Connecticut College
Cornell University
Creighton University
CUNY Hunters College
Dartmouth College
Davidson College
Denison University
DePauw University
Dickinson College
Drexel University
Duke University
Duquesne University
Earlham College
East Carolina University
Elon University
Emerson College
Emory University
FIT
Florida State University
Fordham University

Franklin & Marshall College
Furman University
Geneva College
George Washington University
Georgetown University
Georgia Tech
Gettysburg College
Gonzaga University
Goucher College
Grinnell College
Grove City College
Guilford College
Gustavus Adolphus College
Hamilton College
Hampshire College
Hampton University
Hanover College
Harvard University
Harvey Mudd College
Haverford College
Hofstra University
Hollins University
Howard University
Idaho State University
Illinois State University
Illinois Wesleyan University
Indiana University
Iowa State University
Ithaca College
IUPUI
James Madison University
Johns Hopkins University
Juniata College
Kansas State
Kent State University
Kenyon College
Lafayette College
LaRoche College
Lawrence University
Lehigh University
Lewis & Clark College
Louisiana State University
Loyola College in Maryland
Loyola Marymount University
Loyola University Chicago
Loyola University New Orleans
Macalester College
Marlboro College
Marquette University
McGill University
Miami University of Ohio
Michigan State University
Middle Tennessee State
Middlebury College
Millsaps College
MIT
Montana State University
Mount Holyoke College
Muhlenberg College
New York University
North Carolina State
Northeastern University
Northern Arizona University
Northern Illinois University
Northwestern University
Oberlin College
Occidental College

Ohio State University
Ohio University
Ohio Wesleyan University
Old Dominion University
Penn State University
Pepperdine University
Pitzer College
Pomona College
Princeton University
Providence College
Purdue University
Reed College
Rensselaer Polytechnic Institute
Rhode Island School of Design
Rhodes College
Rice University
Rochester Institute of Technology
Rollins College
Rutgers University
San Diego State University
Santa Clara University
Sarah Lawrence College
Scripps College
Seattle University
Seton Hall University
Simmons College
Skidmore College
Slippery Rock
Smith College
Southern Methodist University
Southwestern University
Spelman College
St. Joseph's University Philladelphia
St. John's University
St. Louis University
St. Olaf College
Stanford University
Stetson University
Stony Brook University
Susquhanna University
Swarthmore College
Syracuse University
Temple University
Tennessee State University
Texas A & M University
Texas Christian University
Towson University
Trinity College Connecticut
Trinity University Texas
Truman State
Tufts University
Tulane University
UC Berkeley
UC Davis
UC Irvine
UC Riverside
UC San Diego
UC Santa Barbara
UC Santa Cruz
UCLA
Union College
University at Albany
University at Buffalo
University of Alabama
University of Arizona
University of Central Florida
University of Chicago

University of Colorado
University of Connecticut
University of Delaware
University of Denver
University of Florida
University of Georgia
University of Illinois
University of Iowa
University of Kansas
University of Kentucky
University of Maine
University of Maryland
University of Massachusetts
University of Miami
University of Michigan
University of Minnesota
University of Mississippi
University of Missouri
University of Nebraska
University of New Hampshire
University of North Carolina
University of Notre Dame
University of Oklahoma
University of Oregon
University of Pennsylvania
University of Pittsburgh
University of Puget Sound
University of Rhode Island
University of Richmond
University of Rochester
University of San Diego
University of San Francisco
University of South Carolina
University of South Dakota
University of South Florida
University of Southern California
University of Tennessee
University of Texas
University of Utah
University of Vermont
University of Virginia
University of Washington
University of Wisconsin
UNLV
Ursinus College
Valparaiso University
Vanderbilt University
Vassar College
Villanova University
Virginia Tech
Wake Forest University
Warren Wilson College
Washington and Lee University
Washington University in St. Louis
Wellesley College
Wesleyan University
West Point
West Virginia University
Wheaton College IL
Wheaton College MA
Whitman College
Wilkes University
Williams College
Xavier University
Yale University